Cracking the GRE Psychology Subject Test

Cracking the GRE Psychology Subject Test

Meg Jay

6TH EDITION

RANDOM HOUSE, INC.
NEW YORK

www.PrincetonReview.com

Princeton Review Publishing, L.L.C.
2315 Broadway
New York, NY 10024
E-mail: booksupport@review.com
Copyright © 2002 by Princeton Review Publishing, L.L.C.

ISBN 0-375-76269-8

Editor: Jeff Soloway
Production Editor: Maria Dente
Production Coordinator: Jennifer Arias

Manufactured in the United States of America.

9 8 7 6 5 4 3

6th Edition

ACKNOWLEDGMENTS

I am indebted to the Berkeley and Boulder offices of The Princeton Review for their ongoing personal and professional support and to the University of California, Berkeley for its massive contribution to my professional development. Also, neither this guide nor its revisions would have been possible without the editors I have worked with over the years, Jeff Soloway, Lesly Atlas and Maria Dente. Many thanks to Dr. Karen Faccenda for her expert review of the manuscript. Finally, my deepest love and gratitude go to my grandmother, and all of the Jays, for teaching me to love education.

Special thanks to Adam Robinson, who conceived of and perfected the Joe Bloggs approach to standardized tests and many of the other successful techniques used by The Princeton Review.

CONTENTS

General Topics

Introduction

IF YOU NEED TO KNOW IT, IT'S IN HERE

Cracking the GRE Psychology Subject Test has been completely updated and revised for its sixth edition to reflect the changing needs of prospective graduate students. To put it mildly, getting into graduate school in psychology is much tougher than it used to be. This book is designed to be the only resource you will need, aside from official literature from schools, the Educational Testing Service (ETS), and the American Psychological Association (APA). You can tackle admissions and the test without gathering a library of books!

THE TEST

This section explains how the GRE Psychology Subject Test works and how you can work aggressively toward a high score. Smart strategy techniques will help you get the most out of what you know (and even what you don't know).

THE MATERIAL

This section has been meticulously researched to include anything that has appeared on past exams, as well as anything so central it could be expected to show up on a future test.

THE PRACTICE TEST

A full-length practice test represents each area that you must know. Use this to determine your strengths and weaknesses.

THE ADMISSIONS PROCESS

This section contains everything you need to know to play the application game.

PART ◆ I

The Test

1

Demystifying the GRE Psychology Subject Test

WHAT IS THE GRE PSYCHOLOGY SUBJECT TEST?

Graduate programs in some fields require a subject test as part of the admission process. Many graduate programs (but not all) in psychology require the GRE Psychology Subject Test, which is comprised of 215 multiple-choice questions from the field of psychology.

Psychology is a wide field, and the questions on the test cover a range of areas. Basically, if you took the final exam for every psychology undergraduate course offered at a major university and randomly selected 215 questions from these exams, you would have the psychology subject test. Yes, it's a lot of material. You should be sure you need to take the test before you prepare.

WHO WRITES THE TEST?

The test is constructed by Educational Testing Service (ETS), the same people who brought you the SAT, the GRE, and other favorites. During test development, academic faculty in psychology are consulted about the content of the questions, but the test is ultimately written by ETS. Don't be intimidated! ETS is a business, not an omniscient educational gatekeeper. ETS also writes tests for barbers, golf pros, and travel agents. The test is a hoop to jump through. Period.

CONTACT INFORMATION

Official ETS information about the GRE Pyschology Subject Test can be found online at www.gre.org. Here's additional contact information for ETS:

Address: GRE-ETS
             P.O. Box 6000
             Princeton, NJ 08541-6000

Phone: 1-609-771-7670
             Monday–Friday 8:00 A.M. – 8:45 P.M. EST (except for U. S. Holidays)
             Fax: 1-609-771-7906

TEST DATES

Currently, the GRE Psychology Subject Test is offered on just three Saturdays throughout the year, in April, November, and December. So it is important to plan to take the test well in advance of any graduate school application to allow yourself the option, if necessary, of retaking the exam.

Note that students claiming special circumstances may request to take the test on the Mondays following each of the Saturday testing dates. Monday testers always receive a different exam, since ETS is always concerned about minimizing any chance of cheating.

TESTING FEE

As of press time, the fee is $130 if you are taking the exam on US soil, and $150 everywhere else in the world. But don't be surprised if it goes up $5 or $10 in the next year or so.

TEST FORMAT

Unlike the General GRE, the GRE Psychology Subject Test is a conventional paper and pencil exams. Each of its 215 multiple-choice questions has five answer choices, (A) through (E), which you select by bubbling in the proper oval on the answer sheet. The permitted testing time is 2 hours 50 minutes.

ON THE DAY OF THE TEST

According to ETS, you should be at the testing center no later than 8:30 AM or else risk being turned away. Plan on being at the testing center for a total of $3\frac{1}{2}$ hours because of extra time required for administrative paperwork associated with the exam. When you're done, go bowling.

Required/Restricted Items on Test Day

You need a bunch of no. 2 pencils and a big eraser. As far as documentation, once you register for the exam, ETS will remind you of the required documentation that you need on test day. Basically, you'll need the registration card that they send you in advance as well as a photo ID with your signature on it, such as a Passport, Driver's License, Military ID, or National ID. If you don't have one of these, pay extra attention to ETS's fine print when you register for the exam to see what you will need to bring instead, otherwise they will have no problem delaying you outside the testing center.

The list of forbidden items is long and glorious and can be found in the GRE registration materials or on the GRE website. But the most important items to mention at this point are: *no calculators*, *no timers that make noise*, and *no headsets*!

SENDING OFF SCORES

When you register for the GRE Psychology Subject Test (and again on the day of the exam), you can list up to four schools that you want ETS to send your scores to for no fee. Having your scores sent to additional schools will cost you $13 per school. Testers receive their scores by mail 6 weeks after the test date.

Note that GRE scores are good for 5 years.

CANCELING SCORES

You can void the exam at any point during the morning of the test. Voiding essentially results in your answer key getting tossed in the trash, and no record of that day ever appears on any future GRE report. Honestly, you should only consider doing this if you're convinced that things have gone seriously wrong (for example, if you have a 104°F fever and have drooled all over the answer sheet, etc.).

TAKING THE TEST MORE THAN ONCE

ETS will let you take the GRE Psychology Subject Test as many times as you want—after all, they make at least $130 a pop. However, since all previous scores show up on the report sent to schools (only voided tests are left off), make every attempt to take the GRE Psychology Subject Test just once. Don't take the test without preparing and consider it just a practice run. Each additional score on your report makes you look more like a professional test taker and less like a potential graduate student.

HOW DOES THE TEST FACTOR INTO THE APPLICATION PROCESS?

The subject tests were created in order to provide graduate admission programs with an indication of an individual's grasp of a particular subject. Of course, for the test you are only expected to have a reasonable undergraduate grasp. You are going to graduate school to learn the most advanced principles. Some schools may use the GRE Psychology Subject Test as an indicator of how well you know psychology, especially if you majored in another field. Other schools may use the test to confirm that you remember what you learned as an undergraduate psychology major. The more competitive schools use the psychology subject test as a factor in screening and competition.

WHAT DOES THE TEST MEASURE?

The GRE Psychology test isn't an indicator of how successful you may be as a psychologist. It is an indicator of how many undergraduate psychology classes you took, how well you remember them, and/or how thoroughly you prepared for the test. Furthermore, because a correlation exists between scores on the GRE Psychology Subject Test and scores on other nonsubject standardized tests, it's clear that the GRE Psychology Subject Test measures general test-taking skills as well.

WHAT MATERIAL DOES IT TEST?

You will be tested on the concepts, specifics, researchers, studies, and principles associated with particular areas. Some of the questions will be general and basic, yet others will be specific and obscure. The areas that you must know:

- **Experimental and Natural Sciences** (about 40% of the 215 total questions)

  Learning (about 10–12 questions)

  Language (about 10–12 questions)

  Memory (about 10–12 questions)

  Cognition (about 10–12 questions)

  Perception (about 10–12 questions)

  Ethology (about 6–8 questions)

  Comparative Psychology (about 6–8 questions)

  Sensation (about 10–12 questions)

  Physiological Psychology (about 10–12 questions)

- **Social and Social Sciences** (about 43% of the 215 total questions)

  Clinical Psychology (about 11–13 questions)

  Abnormal Psychology (about 11–13 questions)

  Developmental Psychology (about 22–30 questions)

  Personality (about 11–20 questions)

  Social Psychology (about 22–30 questions)

- **General Topics** (about 17% of the 215 total questions)

  History of Psychology (about 7 questions)

  Applied Psychology (about 7 questions)

  Measurement (about 7 questions)

  Research Design (about 7 questions)

  Statistics (about 7 questions)

How Does the Test Work?

From your performance on the 215 multiple-choice questions, ETS calculates a raw score, a scaled score, two subscores, and a percentile rank. The scaled score is what schools want.

- **Step 1:** Raw Score

  (Total number of correct responses) − (1/4 of the number you got wrong) = Raw Score

- **Step 2:** Scaled Score

  Your raw score is plugged into a conversion chart that assigns it a value between 200 and 900. This is your scaled score, and the score that interests graduate schools. The conversion charts vary slightly per test due to small variations in test difficulty.

- **Step 3:** Subscores

  Subscore I reflects your performance on questions from the Experimental and Natural Sciences category. Subscore II reflects your performance on questions from the Social and Social Sciences category. Subscores range from 20–99 although the extremes are very rare. These subscores, though present on your ETS score report, are basically ignored by graduate programs.

- **Step 4:** Percentile Rank

  Your percentile is calculated by comparing your raw score to that of others who took that test and other recent psychology subject tests. Your percentile rank indicates what percentage of students scored lower than you did.

Example:

Let's say that after completing the 215 questions, you got 125 correct and 90 incorrect. Your raw score would be 125 − (90/4) or 125 − 22.5. This yields a raw score of 102.5, which is rounded to the nearest whole number, 103. The conversion table printed to the right provides approximate conversions to scaled scores and percentiles. From the chart, you would have scored a 540 and a 39 percent rank.

What Score Do I Need?

GRE Psychology scaled scores fall between 250 and 840. Extreme scores are so rare that a score of about 750 or above places you in the 99th percentile. Generally, schools want to see a scaled score between 550 and 650. The mean score of *admitted* students, however, is often in the 600–700 range, depending on the program. It is difficult to generalize about scores needed for admission because of the many varying psychology programs. Some programs will accept scores in the 400s and 500s. More competitive schools boast average scores in the high 700s. The program literature for a particular school will clearly state the GRE Psychology Subject Test scores preferred for that program.

When determining your score goal, there are two ways to go. One way is to take a practice GRE Psychology Subject Test (the best is the real ETS test you can download for free a www.gre.org) and calculate your score. Think realistically about how much time you have to study and create a score goal for yourself. Score improvements vary drastically depending mostly on study time and familiarity with the material. If this is your plan, after the actual test, you will go shopping for graduate programs based on the score you received.

The second way is to look at the scores for admitted applicants of those programs that interest you. These are the scores that you need. Take an ETS psychology practice test, see where you are, and plan to study accordingly. Though improvement is all about preparation, don't forget to be realistic.

Score Conversions for GRE Psychology Subject Test Subscores TOTAL SCORE					
Raw Score	Scaled Score	%	Raw Score	Scaled Score	%
211-214	840	99	103-106	540	39
207-210	830	99	100-102	530	36
204-206	820	99	96-99	520	32
200-203	810	99	93-95	510	29
197-199	800	99	89-92	500	26
193-196	790	99	85-88	490	22
189-192	780	99	82-84	480	20
186-188	770	99	78-81	470	17
182-185	760	98	75-77	460	14
179-181	750	97	71-74	450	12
175-178	740	96	67-70	440	10
172-174	730	95	64-66	430	9
168-171	720	94	60-63	420	7
164-167	710	92	57-59	410	6
161-163	700	90	53-56	400	4
157-160	690	88	50-52	390	4
154-156	680	86	46-49	370	2
150-153	670	84	39-41	360	2
146-149	660	81	35-38	350	1
143-145	650	78	32-34	340	1
139-142	640	75	28-31	330	1
136-138	630	72	24-27	320	1
132-135	620	68	21-23	310	1
128-131	610	65	17-20	300	1
125-127	600	62			
121-124	590	58	14-16	290	1
118-120	580	54	10-13	280	1
114-117	570	50	6-9	270	1
111-113	560	47	3-5	260	1
107-110	550	43	0-2	250	1

TOP 10 WAYS TO PREPARE

Gone are the days when subject tests were perceived as tests of general knowledge. If it were that easy, we would all get 700s! With the keen competition for positions in psychology graduate programs, the GRE Psychology Subject Test has moved beyond functioning as a simple achievement indicator. Yikes! What do you do?

1. Use the practice test in this book to gauge your baseline knowledge. Let questions you miss point out your weak areas. Though our test has been designed to mirror the structure and content of the actual test, consider your performance only an approximation.

2. Learn this book. We know you don't need to do okay on the GRE Psychology Test— you need to do really well. So guess what? It's all in here! The material in this book either appeared on an old test or is so central to the subject that it is expected to appear on a future test.

3. Study frequently. Humans learn best in short, spaced, frequent intervals. Most people take at least 6 weeks to prepare for the GRE Psychology Test. Just say no to cramming.

4. Practice pop psychology on yourself. Stop imagining the worst and envision the best. Don't let the test make you feel like a deer in the headlights! Study and feel confident that you are prepared.

5. Use the smart test-taking techniques that we teach in chapter 2. Get points even when you don't know the answer. Take the test, don't let the test take you!

6. Obtain a copy of an ETS Practice GRE Psychology Subject Test. An official ETS practice test will be sent to you for free when you register to take the test. You can also download it from the GRE website at www.gre.org. Taking an *actual* old test like this one is absolutely, positively the best way to estimate your score. An ETS test will accurately reflect how much you have learned and what areas still need work.

7. Stay away from books not published by ETS that offer endless practice questions. These books contain questions that are either too hard or too easy, or may be downright inappropriate. Your time is best spent studying rather than answering bad questions.

8. Don't be a perfectionist. You cannot know everything. No matter how hard you study, the test will include researchers, terms, and principles that you have never heard of. It's okay. Certain questions are designed to weed people out.

9. Okay, if you *must* be a perfectionist, then the Internet can help you. In this book, concepts and studies are described in the most economical way possible—that is, with the least amount of detail. If every concept were explained in depth, then this guide would be overwhelming. In general, concepts that are given little attention (perhaps a bullet-point or two) have shown up on some (but not all) recent tests in the form of one question. Concepts that are discussed in more detail usually receive attention on every test administration. If a bullet-point or an explanation does not meet your satisfaction, search for the term on the Internet. Many websites related to psychology and research will explain terms in more depth.

10. Students often ask me what in this book is important. Well, everything! Absolutely everything in this guide has appeared on a recent test; in other words, nothing in this book is included just for the fun of it. But, of course, not everyone needs or wants a 750, so study accordingly. If you are hoping to cram and squeak by, then study the concepts discussed in detail that comprise the bulk of chapters; also notice the relative percentage of coverage that each area typically receives on tests (for example, social psychology is much more important to your score than ethology). If you need to do really well on the subject test, then start early and try to learn everything in this book.

2

Short Cuts

GETTING THE MOST OUT OF WHAT YOU KNOW

On the GRE Psychology Subject Test, the issue is not so much pacing as it is accuracy. Given the 170-minute time limit, most people find that they are able to finish the test. They just wish that more of their answers were correct. With simple techniques, you can maximize what you know.

DO YOU WANT MY BEST GUESS?

To guess or not to guess, that is the question. The GRE Psychology Subject Test is scored using a guessing correction technique. This guessing correction is the part in the scoring when ETS subtracts 1/4 of your incorrect responses from the number of your correct responses. They figure that you got some random guesses correct, and they want to take these points away from you. Let's say that you randomly guessed "D" for 30 questions. Statistically speaking, "D" should be correct about 1/5 of the time because there are have 5 answer choices for each question. So, of these 30 random guesses, you would get 1/5, or 6, of those correct. Now, you have at least 24 remaining incorrect answer choices, and 1/4 of those (6 in this case) are subtracted from your score. So they took away your lucky guesses. It would seem that random guessing is a wash. But what about guessing that is not *completely* random? This is another matter. With every answer choice that you are able to cross off through Process of Elimination, you are increasing the likelihood that your guess will be correct. This means that your guess is not entirely random, so you are beating the statistics of the guessing correction.

> **If you eliminate even *one* of the choices, you are beating the odds, so GUESS.**

BIG PICTURE TEST STRATEGY

For purposes of technique, the questions on the psychology test can be divided into three types:

- Ones you **know** the answer to

- Ones you **sort of know** the answer to

- Ones you have **no idea** about

We recommend that test-takers use a **three-pass system** on the GRE Psychology Subject Test. What this means is that you go through the test and first answer all of the questions for which you are sure of the answer. Then, you take another whirl with the leftover questions and use aggressive techniques in order to make an informed and educated guess on the questions you "sort of" know the answers to. Finally, you deal with the questions you have no clue about. It is senseless to run out of time because you struggled with harder questions while you could have been answering easier ones. Take all the points you can get and then struggle with what's left.

FIRST PASS: YOU KNOW THE ANSWER, YOU SEE IT, YOU CIRCLE IT, YOU MOVE ON

On your first run through the test, read all of the questions and answer the giveaways. Don't waste time struggling with confusing questions when you could be racking up points. After you are done with the easy questions, you'll know how much time is left for the others. As you skip questions, circle the ones you think you can work with. Put a question mark by questions that you have no idea about.

SECOND PASS: GUESS AGGRESSIVELY (NOT RANDOMLY)

Now, you work with the questions that you sort of know the answer to—the ones you circled on the first pass. For these questions, you have a good shot of beating the odds of the guessing correction. You'll need to be active and involved with the question and the answers. Guessing aggressively requires skill.

- **Process of Elimination** is your best friend here. Even if you don't figure out what the right answer is, by ruling out choices that you know are incorrect, you increase the probability that your guess will be correct.

- **Use common sense.** Luckily, psychology is a relatively modern field with relatively practical principles. Subject tests do not try to trick you. (Sometimes you can even find unintended hints to the answer within the question and answer choices.) The subject material on the test is considered important (not wacky or random) by faculty consultants. Psychology terms often mean what they sound like. Use this to your advantage. If you do not know the answer to a question but can make a logical guess, go for it! Here's how this works. . .

> 56. According to Maslow's hierarchy of needs, the most basic human needs are
>
> (A) food and water
> (B) a safe place to live
> (C) the love and esteem of others
> (D) self-actualization
> (E) intellectual challenge

Some questions are this basic, yet seem difficult because you're not up on your Maslow. But Maslow fan or not, a good guess is that our most basic needs are food and water.

47. Which of the following are newborn infants
    unable to see?

    (A) simple shapes
    (B) vivid colors
    (C) weak light
    (D) intense contrasts
    (E) intricate detail

Because the question implies that babies do not have great eyesight, think about sight logically. Of the five answer choices, what would be the easiest things to distinguish? Probably (A), (B), and (D), so eliminate those. (If you guess now, you have a 50 percent chance of getting the right answer.) Between (C) and (E), do you have a guess as to what would be the most difficult thing to see? If you guessed (E) you're right.

• **Sesame Street the EXCEPT questions.**

One of these things is not like the others.

One of these things is not the same.

Well, can you guess which thing is not like the others?

That's how we play this game.

Sesame Street is so educational that it will even help you on your subject test! Some questions on the test will be what we call "EXCEPT" questions. They are easy to spot because they contain EXCEPT, LEAST, or NOT in big letters. The key to answering these questions is to think of the answer you want as the odd man out. It will be out of step somehow with the other four choices. So even if you don't know the answer to the question being asked, you can guess aggressively using the Sesame Street technique. Let's play. . .

107. Damage to the hypothalamus would be likely
     to impair each of the following EXCEPT:

     (A) sexual behavior
     (B) aggression
     (C) vision
     (D) temperature control
     (E) hunger

So you didn't get around to learning your physiology for the test. What do you do? Look for one thing different from the rest! (A) and (B) both seem like basic elements of instinct or survival. Not the case with (C). (D) and (E) seem necessary for survival. (C) is the oddball and, for our purposes, the answer we want.

- **Go with what you know.** The GRE Psychology Subject Test is not a trick! It is supposed to measure your knowledge about important principles in the field, not about unimportant hocus-pocus. The rule is simple: If all else fails, just choose the answer you have heard of.

THIRD PASS: DON'T BOTHER WITH RANDOM GUESSES

Only after you have answered all of the questions you know and sort of know, do you spend your time on questions that you have no idea about. If time is remaining, take another look at the questions that you put question marks next to. If you can eliminate at least one answer choice, take a guess. If it is a blind guess, leave it blank.

MORAL OF THE STORY

You do not have to know everything to get a good score on the psychology test! First, take another look at the conversion chart. You can answer 80 wrong and still score in the 600s! Second, you don't have to know the answer to a question in order to answer it correctly. Using the techniques that we've provided, you can beat the odds of the guessing correction. Every little bit counts!

PART ◆ **II**

The Material

3

Learning

DEFINED: Learning is the relatively permanent or stable change in behavior as the result of experience. That much is agreed upon, but different people have different ideas about exactly why and how animals learn. Some theorists assert that animals learn in order to manipulate rewards and punishments. Others believe that animals learn through temporal relationships or pairing. Most likely, many types of learning come into play at different points.

BIG WIGS

- **E. L. Thorndike** suggested the **Law of Effect**, which was the precursor of operant conditioning. The Law of Effect postulated a cause and effect chain of behavior revolving around reinforcement. Individuals do what rewards them and stop doing what doesn't bring some reward.

- **Kurt Lewin** developed the **Theory of Association,** which was a forerunner of behaviorism. Association is grouping things together based on the fact that they occur together in time and space. Organisms associate certain behaviors with certain rewards and certain cues with certain situations. This idea is basically what Ivan Pavlov later proved experimentally. (See also Social Psychology.)

- **Ivan Pavlov** was first famous as the winner of a Nobel Prize for work on digestion. During more work investigating dogs and digestion, he quite accidentally uncovered the concept now called classical conditioning. **Classical conditioning**, also known as **Pavlovian conditioning**, involves teaching an organism to respond to a neutral stimulus by pairing the neutral stimulus with a not-so-neutral stimulus. Pavlov knew he was on to something when his dogs would salivate not just at the sight of food but also at the sound of his assistant's footsteps. The neutral stimulus of the footsteps had been paired so often with the arrival of food that the dogs began to salivate simply in response to the footsteps.

- **John B. Watson** expanded the ideas of Pavlov and founded the **school of behaviorism**. Watson's idea of learning, like his idea of all behavior, was that everything could be explained by stimulus-response chains and that conditioning was the key factor in developing these chains. Only objective and observable elements were of importance to organisms and to psychology.

- **B. F. Skinner** conducted the first scientific experiments to prove the concepts in Thorndike's Law of Effect and in Watson's idea of the causes and effects of behavior. This idea of behavior being influenced primarily by reinforcement is now called **operant conditioning**. Skinner practically created the now classic stereotype of psychological study; he used rats and a device that he created called the **Skinner box**. Experimentally, Skinner proved that animals are influenced by reinforcement. Later, Skinner went even further in his famous books *Walden Two* and *Beyond Freedom and Dignity* by discussing the control of human behavior rather than rat behavior.

Classical Conditioning

Classical conditioning is one of psychology's most famous learning principles. Classical conditioning, pioneered by Pavlov, is often called Pavlovian conditioning. This type of conditioning involves pairing a neutral stimulus with a not-so-neutral stimulus; this creates a relationship between the two. As discussed above, Pavlov noticed that his dogs salivated when they heard the footsteps of his assistant. To test his theory that the dogs had inferred a relationship from these temporal events, Pavlov attempted to teach his dogs to salivate to an even more neutral stimulus: a light. In order to set up a relationship between food and a particular light, Pavlov arranged for a certain light to be turned on just prior to the dogs' being fed. After consistent pairings of these two stimuli (the neutral stimuli of the light and the not-so-neutral stimuli of the food), the dogs would salivate in the presence of either. Of course, food still elicited saliva, but more importantly, the dogs began to salivate even when just the light was turned on.

Classical conditioning is pretty easy to understand, but unfortunately, all of the vocabulary is not. Classical conditioning lingo is both important and plentiful on the GRE Psychology Subject Test. These first four concepts are crucial:

Unconditioned stimulus (UCS)

The not-so-neutral stimulus. In Pavlov's dog experiments, the UCS is the food. Without conditioning, the stimulus elicits the response of salivating.

Conditioned stimulus (CS)

The neutral stimulus that is paired with the UCS. The CS has no naturally occurring response, but it is conditioned through pairings with a UCS. In classical conditioning, a CS (the light) is paired with a UCS (food), so that the CS alone will produce a response.

Unconditioned response (UCR)

The naturally occurring response to the UCS.

Conditioned response (CR)

The response that the CS elicits after conditioning. The UCR and the CR are the same (salivating to food or a light, for example).

Next, we have a barrage of words that relate to the different orders and ways in which one could present the UCS and CS within classical conditioning.

Simultaneous conditioning

The UCS and CS are presented at the same time.

Higher-order conditioning/second-order conditioning

A conditioning technique in which a previous CS now acts as a UCS. Using Pavlov's dogs as an example, for higher-order conditioning, the experimenter would use the light as a UCS after the light reliably elicited saliva in the dogs. Food would no longer be used in the experiment, but now, the light would be the UCS. The light could be paired with a bell (CS) until the bell alone elicited saliva in the dogs.

Forward conditioning

Pairing of the CS and the UCS in which the CS is presented before the UCS. Two types of forward conditioning are delayed conditioning and trace conditioning:

- **Delayed conditioning.** The presentation of the CS begins before that of the UCS and lasts until the UCS is presented.

- **Trace conditioning.** The CS stimulus is presented and terminated before the UCS is presented.

Backward conditioning

The CS is presented after the UCS is presented. For Pavlov's dogs, they would have been presented with the food and then with the light. Backward conditioning has proven to be ineffective. In fact, it accomplishes only **inhibitory conditioning**, which means that later the dogs would have a harder time pairing the light and the food even if they were presented in a forward fashion.

OPERANT CONDITIONING

Operant conditioning, also called **instrumental conditioning**, was pioneered by B. F. Skinner. Operant conditioning aims to influence a response through various reinforcement strategies. Basically, it's the idea that we do what reaps rewards and vice versa. Skinner is most famous for his initial studies, in which he used rats and his device, the Skinner box. This box was basically bare on the inside except for a lever and a hole through which food pellets were inserted. Though many different reinforcement schedules were used, the basic idea is that the rats repeated behaviors that won them rewards and gave up on behaviors that did not.

Courtesy Nina Leen © Time Inc.

B. F. Skinner (1904–1990)

In Skinner's experiments, the goal was to condition the rats to perform an unnatural behavior: pressing the lever in the Skinner box. The plan was to accomplish this through reinforcement of such behavior. The first problem was getting the rats to press the lever.

Courtesy Susan M. Hogue

. . . and two of his unpaid assistants

Through a process called **shaping**, the experimenter rewarded the rats (with food pellets) for even being near the lever and then rewarded them again for touching the lever. The rats were rewarded for behaviors that brought them closer and closer to actually pressing the bar. Thus, another term for shaping is the **differential reinforcement of successive approximations.** Eventually, this led the rats to the desired behavior of pressing the bar. At that point, only bar pressing was rewarded. These rats were successfully operantly conditioned.

Skinner and others since have tested various reinforcement strategies. Here's some operant vocabulary that you should know:

Primary reinforcement

A natural reinforcement. Something that is reinforcing on its own without the requirement of learning. Food and water are primary reinforcers.

Secondary reinforcement

A learned reinforcer. Money is the perfect example. Every day, we work to be rewarded with money, but for someone on a desert island, money would do very little. Secondary reinforcements are often learned through society. Other examples are prestige, awards, and a token economy.

Positive reinforcement

A type of reward or positive event acting as a stimulus that increases the likelihood of a particular response. Rewarding a dog with a treat stimulates the response of obeying in the future. Some subjects are not motivated by rewards because they don't believe or understand that the rewards will be given.

Negative reinforcement

Negative reinforcement is not punishment. It is not the delivery of a negative consequence. Rather, it is reinforcement through the removal of a negative event. If a monkey in a cage were subjected to a blaring noise at all times, except when the monkey rode a tricycle, the monkey would learn to ride the tricycle more often in order to stop the noise. In negative reinforcement, the stimulus is the removal of something negative.

There are two essential differences between negative reinforcement and punishment: first, negative reinforcement encourages the subject to behave a certain way, and punishment encourages a subject to *stop* behaving in a certain way; and second, negative reinforcement entails removing a negative event, and punishment entails introducing a negative event. Skinner did not use punishment, as he felt it was not effective.

Continuous reinforcement schedule

In this schedule, every correct response is met with some form of reinforcement. This type of reinforcement strategy facilitates the quickest learning, but also the most fragile learning; as soon as the rewards stop coming, the animal stops performing.

Partial reinforcement schedules

In this schedule, not all correct responses are met with reinforcement. This strategy may require a longer learning time, but once learned, these behaviors are more resistant to extinction. There are four distinct types of partial reinforcement schedules:

1. **Fixed ratio schedule**. In this schedule, a reinforcement is delivered after a consistent number of responses. If the ratio is 6:1, after every 6 correct responses, there is a reward. The power of drug addiction has been proven using this schedule. Drug addicted rats in a Skinner box-type apparatus will press a bar vigorously and consistently upon discovering that after every few pressings a drug is delivered. Because the ratio is fixed, the behavior is vulnerable to extinction. When the rewards stop coming as scheduled, the animal will discern this and give up on receiving the rewards.

2. **Variable ratio schedule.** In this schedule, learning takes the most time to occur, but the learning is least likely to become extinguished. A variable ratio is different than a fixed ratio schedule in that reinforcements are delivered after different numbers of correct responses. The ratio cannot be predicted. Slot machines are the perfect example of this strategy. The gambler is rewarded every so often, but there is no way to tell if the reward is only one coin away or two days away. Las Vegas was built on the variable ratio strategy.

3. **Fixed interval schedule.** A fixed interval schedule does little to motivate an animal's behavior. With interval schedules, rewards come after the passage of a certain period of time, regardless of any behaviors from the animal. Some argue that salaried employees and tenured professors are beneficiaries of this uninspiring strategy. Paychecks come every two weeks, no matter what one does.

4. **Variable interval schedule.** In this schedule, rewards are delivered after differing time periods. Variable interval schedule is the second most effective strategy in maintaining behavior. The length of time varies, so one never knows when the reinforcement is just around the corner. Waiting for a bus is a good example. Even though there's nothing we can do to make the bus arrive earlier, we tend to wait because we never know when the bus might arrive.

Token economy

An artificial mini-economy is usually found in prisons, rehabilitation centers, or mental hospitals. Individuals in the environment are motivated by secondary reinforcers, tokens in this case. Desirable behaviors are reinforced with tokens, which can be cashed in for more primary reinforcers, such as candy, books, privileges, or cigarettes.

MOTIVATION AND PERFORMANCE

An animal must be motivated in order to learn and to act. Individuals are at times motivated by **primary** or **instinctual drives**, such as hunger or thirst. Other times, they are motivated by **secondary** or **acquired** drives, such as money or other learned reinforcers. Still other types of drive, such as an **exploratory drive**, may exist. Experiments have shown that individuals are motivated simply to try something new or to explore their environment. Various theories of motivation exist:

- Some theories assert that humans are primarily motivated to maintain physiological or psychological **homeostasis**. **Fritz Heider's Balance Theory, Charles Osgood** and **Percy Tannenbaum's Congruity Theory,** and **Leon Festinger's Cognitive Dissonance Theory** (see Social Psychology) all agree that what drives people is a desire to be balanced with respect to their feelings, ideas, or behaviors. These theories, along with **drive-reduction theories**, are called into question by the fact that individuals often seek out stimulation, novel experience, or self-destruction.

- **Clark Hull** proposed that **Performance = Drive $\times$ Habit**. This means that individuals are first motivated by drive, and then they act according to old successful habits. They will do what has worked in the past to satisfy the drive.

- **Edward Tolman** proposed that **Performance = Expectation $\times$ Value**. This is also known as the **Expectancy-Value Theory**. The idea here is that people are motivated by goals that they think they might actually meet. Another factor is how important the goal is. **Victor Vroom** applied this theory to individual behavior in large organizations. Individuals who are lowest on the totem pole do not expect to receive company incentives, so these carrots do little to motivate them.

- **Henry Murray** and later **David McClelland** studied the possibility that people are motivated by a **need for achievement (nAch)**. This may be manifested through a need to pursue success or a need to avoid failure, but either way, the goal is to feel successful. Also, **John Atkinson** suggested a theory of motivation in which people set realistic goals with intermediate risk sets feel pride with accomplishment, and want to succeed more than they fear failure. But because success is so important, these people are unlikely to set unrealistic or risky goals or to persist when success is unlikely.

- **Neil Miller** proposed the **approach-avoidance conflict**. This conflict refers to the state one feels when a certain goal has both pros and cons. Typically, the further one is from the goal, the more one focuses on the pros or the reasons to approach the goal. The closer one is to the goal, the more one focuses on the cons or the reasons to avoid the goal.

- **Hedonism** is the theory that individuals are motivated solely by what brings the most pleasure and the least pain.

- **The Premack Principle** is the idea that people are motivated to do what they do not want to do by rewarding themselves afterward with something they like to do. For example, a young child may be rewarded with dessert only after he eats his spinach.

Arousal is a part of motivation, and an individual must be adequately aroused to learn or perform. **Donald Hebb** postulated that a medium amount of arousal is best for performance. Too little arousal or too much arousal could hamper performance of tasks. Specifically, for simple tasks, the optimal level of arousal is toward the high end. For complex tasks, the optimal level of arousal is toward the low end, so that the individual is not too anxious to perform well. The optimal arousal level for any type of task, however, is never at the extremes. The above relationship is the **Yerkes-Dodson Effect**. On a graph, optimal arousal looks like an inverted U-curve, with lowest performance at the extremes of arousal.

OTHER THINGS YOU SHOULD KNOW

- **Stimulus** refers to any event that an organism reacts to. The stimulus is the first link in a stimulus-response chain.

- **Stimulus discrimination** refers to the ability to discriminate between different but similar stimuli. Every day, we react to discriminated stimuli. A doorbell ringing means something different from a phone ringing. An ice cream truck's tune means something different from a car stereo heard from a passing car.

- **Stimulus generalization** is the opposite of **stimulus discrimination**. To generalize is to make the same response to a group of similar stimuli. Though not all fire alarms sound alike, we know that they all require the same response. **Undergeneralization** is the failure to generalize a stimulus.

- **Response learning** refers to the form of learning in which one links together chains of stimuli and responses. One learns *what* to do in response to particular triggers. An example of response learning is leaving a building in response to a fire alarm.

- **Perceptual** or **concept learning** refers to learning about something in general rather than learning-specific stimulus-response chains. An individual learns *about* something (history, for example) rather than any particular response. **Tolman's** experiments with animals forming **cognitive maps** of mazes rather than simple escape routes are an example of this.

- **Aversive conditioning** uses negative reinforcement to control behavior. An animal is motivated to perform a certain behavior in order to escape or avoid a negative stimulus.

- **Avoidance conditioning** teaches an animal how to avoid something the animal does not want.

- **Escape conditioning** teaches an animal to perform a desired behavior to get away from a negative stimulus.

- **Punishment** promotes extinction of an undesirable behavior. After an unwanted behavior is performed, the punishment is presented. This acts as a negative stimulus, which should decrease the likelihood that the earlier behavior will be repeated. Of course, punishment has received mixed reviews. Some animal experiments have shown that severe punishment effectively extinguishes undesirable behavior. Many, including Skinner himself, argue that punishment is not effective in the long run because it carries with it too many negative effects.

- **Autonomic conditioning** refers to evoking responses of the autonomic nervous system through training.

- **State dependent learning** refers to the concept that what a person learns in one state is best recalled in that state. State, here, is obviously referring to a physiological state, not the united fifty.

- **Extinction** is the reversal of conditioning. The goal is to encourage an organism to stop doing a particular behavior. This is generally accomplished by repeatedly withholding reinforcement for a behavior or by disassociating the behavior from a particular cue. Using operant conditioning, parents can reduce temper tantrums in children by not giving into, or reinforcing, the child's behavior. Using classical conditioning, you could teach your dog to disassociate the car from the vet by taking it on frequent car trips to the park.

- **Latent learning** takes place even without reinforcement. The actual learning is revealed at some other time. For example, maybe you have watched someone play chess many times. The fact that you are learning while watching may not be evident, but when you play chess later, you find that you have learned some new tricks.

- **Incidental learning** is like accidental learning. Unrelated items are grouped together during incidental learning. For example, pets often learn to dislike riding in cars because it means they are going to the vet. Though it is actually the vet that the animal fears, pets associate cars with the vet experience. Incidental learning is the opposite of **intentional learning**.

- **Chaining** is the act of linking together a series of behaviors that ultimately result in reinforcement. One behavior triggers the next and so on. Learning the alphabet is an example of chaining. Twenty-six letters are required to complete the chain, and each letter stimulates remembering the next letter.

- **Habituation** is the decreasing responsiveness to a stimulus as a result of increasing familiarity with the stimulus.

- **Spontaneous recovery** is the reappearance of an extinguished response, even in the absence of further conditioning or training.

- **Overshadowing** is a classical conditioning concept referring to an animal's inability to infer a relationship between a particular stimulus and response due to the presence of a more prominent stimulus.

- **Sensitization** is increased sensitivity to the environment following the presentation of a strong stimulus.

- **Autoshaping** refers to experiments in which an apparatus allows an animal to control its reinforcements through behaviors, such as bar pressing or key pecking. The animal is, in a sense, shaping its own behavior.

- **Social learning theory** posits that individuals learn through their culture. People learn what are acceptable and unacceptable behaviors through interacting in society.

- **Modeling** is a specific concept within **social learning**. Conveniently named, modeling refers to learning and behaving by imitating others. A particularly famous study of modeling was performed by **Albert Bandura** using the **BoBo doll**. In this study, children who watched adults physically abuse a blowup doll in a playroom proceeded to do the same during their playtime with the BoBo doll; children who did not witness the aggression did not behave in this way.

- **Observational learning** is simply the act of learning something by watching.

- **John Garcia** performed classical conditioning experiments in which it was discovered that animals are programmed through evolution to make certain connections. Evolution imposed limitations on what associations animals would make. Garcia studied "conditioned nausea" with rats and found that invariably nausea was perceived to be connected with food or drink. Garcia was unable to condition a relationship between nausea and a neutral stimulus (like a light). This extremely strong connection that animals form between nausea and food has been used to explain why we can become sick only one time from eating a particular food and never be able to eat that food again; the connection is automatic, so it needs little conditioning. This phenomenon is called the **Garcia Effect** and is especially strong in children.

- **M. E. Olds** performed experiments in which electrical stimulation of pleasure centers in the brain were used as positive reinforcement. Animals would perform behaviors to receive the stimulation. This was viewed as evidence against the **drive-reduction theory**.

- The **Hull-Spence** theory of learning hypothesizes that animals learn to respond differently to different stimuli. This is a theory of **discrimination learning.**

- **Continuous** motor tasks are easier to learn than **discrete** motor tasks. An example of a continuous task is riding a bicycle. This is one continuous motion that, once you get started, is natural to continue. A discrete task is one that is divided into different parts that do not facilitate the recall of each other. Setting up a chessboard is a good example. Placing the different pieces in their proper positions involves different bits of information. This is not one unbroken task.

Bandura's widely-cited "BoBo doll" study
(A) provided support for the views of social learning theorists
(B) taught children to defend themselves against killer clowns

Answer: (A)

- **Positive transfer** is previous learning that makes it easier to learn another task later. Previous learning that makes it more difficult to learn a new task is called **negative transfer**.

- **Age** has been shown to affect learning. Humans are primed to learn between the ages of 3 and 20 (the school years). From the age of 20 to 50, the ability to learn remains fairly constant. After the age of 50, the ability to learn drops.

Study Tip: The best way to learn a task is by practicing or by studying in short, frequent intervals. People learn better if they study for a while, take a break, and then study again. So, just say no to cramming!

4

Language

DEFINED: Language is the meaningful arrangement of sounds. Psycholinguistics is the study of the psychology of language. Luckily, psycholinguistics is a highly specialized area of research in which only a limited number of concepts relate to general psychology. For this reason, the language topics that might be covered on the GRE Psychology Subject Test are predictable.

BASIC TERMS

- **Phonemes.** Discrete sounds that make up words but carry no meaning, such as "ee," "p," or "sh." Infants first make these sounds when learning language. Phonics is learning to read by sounding out the phonemes. All words in a language are created from basic phonological rules of sound combination.

- **Morphemes.** Made up of phonemes; the smallest units of meaning in language. Words or parts of words that have meaning are morphemes. The word "boy" and the suffix "-ing" are morphemes.

- **Syntax.** The arrangement of words into sentences as prescribed by a particular language.

- **Grammar.** The overall rules of the interrelationship between morphemes and syntax that make up a certain language.

- **Morphology** or **Morphological rules.** Grammar rules; how to group morphemes.

- **Prosody.** Tone inflections, accents, and other aspects of pronunciation that carry meaning. Prosody is the icing on the cake of grammar and meaning. Infants can more easily differentiate between completely different sounds than between different expressions of the same sound.

NOAM CHOMSKY

Noam Chomsky is undoubtedly the most important figure in psycholinguistics. You will see at least one or two questions about his work. Chomsky's **transformational grammar** differentiates between surface structure and deep structure in language. **Surface structure** is the way that words are organized. Each of the following sentences has a different surface structure:

> I studied the material for hours.
> The material was studied for hours by me.
> For hours, I studied the material.

But the **deep structure** or the underlying meaning of the above sentences is the same. Each of those sentences has the same active declarative kernel sentence (subject = I, verb = studied, object = material).

Probably Chomsky's most famous contribution to psycholinguistics was his idea of an innate **Language Acquisition Device (LAD)**. After studying children and noticing how they made small errors ("I founded the toy") often based on grammar rules rather than large structural errors, Chomsky proposed that humans have an inborn ability to adopt generative grammar rules of the language that they hear. The rules are then used to make millions of novel sentences.

One reason that the LAD is so important and controversial is that it is a nativist or genetic interpretation. According to Chomsky, children need only be exposed to a language in order to easily apply the LAD. They do not simply imitate, memorize, or learn through conditioning. The LAD also explains why children who are learning different languages progress similarly.

OTHER THINGS YOU SHOULD KNOW

- **Overregularization** is the over-application of grammar rules. For example, children realize that past tense is indicated by the suffix "-ed." Then they add this to verbs that don't actually need it, as in the sentence "I founded the toy." Also, children think that plural always requires "-s," as in "sheeps." Even after a child correctly learns an adult speech pattern, such as saying "sheep" instead of "sheeps," he periodically slips back into old errors.

- **Overextension** is generalizing with names for things. This is often done through chaining characteristics rather than through logic. For example, a three year old may call any furry thing a "doggie."

- **Telegraphic speech** refers to speech without the articles or extras, similar to how it would appear in a telegram, such as "Me go."

- **Holophrastic speech** is when a young child uses one word (**holophrases**) to convey a whole sentence. "Me" may mean "give that to me."

- **Girls** are faster and more accurate with language learning than **boys** are.

- **Bilingual children** are slower at language learning.

- **Language acquisition milestones:**

    - 1 year   speaks first word(s)

    - 2 years   > 50 spoken words, usually in two-(and then three-) word phrases

    - 3 years   1,000 word vocabulary, but use has many grammatical errors

    - 4 years   grammar problems are random exceptions

- **Benjamin Whorf** (from studies of Hopi language) posited that language, or how a culture says things, influences that culture's perspective. This **Whorfian Hypothesis** has been used as an argument for the importance of nonsexist language. It has been found, however, that cultures that don't have words for certain colors can still recognize them, so it is unclear to what extent language really affects our perceptions.

- **Roger Brown** researched the areas of social, developmental, and linguistic psychology. He found that children's understanding of grammatical rules develops as they make hypotheses about how syntax works and then self-correct with experience.

- **Katherine Nelson** found that language really begins to develop with the onset of **active speech** rather than during the first year of only listening.

- **William Labov** studied "Black" English (now known as Ebonics) and found that it had its own complex internal structure. It is not simply incorrect English.

- **Leo Vygotsky** and **Alexander Luria**, Russia's best-known psychologists, studied the development of word meanings and found them to be complex and altered by interpersonal experience. Also, they asserted that language is a tool involved in (not just a byproduct of) the development of abstract thinking.

- **Charles Osgood** studied semantics, or word meanings. He created **semantic differential charts**, which allowed people to plot the meanings of words on graphs (like near "good" but far from "relaxed"). The results were that people with similar backgrounds and interests plotted words similarly. This indicates that words have similar **connotations** (implied meaning) for cultures or subcultures.

Study Tip: **Verbalization** (saying things out loud) helps learning.

5
Memory

DEFINED: Studying memory involves understanding how things are remembered and why things are forgotten.

STAGES OF MEMORY

There are three stages of memory—sensory, short term, and long term.

SENSORY MEMORY

- Lasts only for seconds.

- Forms the connection between perception and memory.

- **Iconic memory** is the sensory memory for vision studied by **George Sperling**. He found that people could see more than they can remember. In his classic experiment, subjects were shown something like this for a fraction of a second:

  GPRZ
  ILTH
  TBAE

  Then they were instructed to write down the letters of a particular line. Although subjects were able to do this, they invariably forgot the other letters in the time that it took to write the first ones down. This **partial report** shows that sensory memory exists, but only for a few seconds.

- **Ulric Neisser** coined the term **icon** for brief visual memory and found that an icon lasts for about one second. In addition, he found that when subjects are exposed to a bright flash of light or a new pattern before the iconic image fades, the first image will be erased. This is **backward masking,** and it works for the auditory system as well. A mask is more successful if it is similar to the original stimulus.

- The concept of sensory memory explains why, if you wiggle a pen back and forth, you see trails or a ghost pen in all positions. The sensory information remains briefly in your awareness, and because the pen moves quickly, the information all runs together.

- **Echoic memory** is the sensory memory for auditory sensations.

Short-Term Memory (STM)

- Temporary; lasts for seconds or minutes.

- **George Miller** found that short-term memory has the capacity of about 7 items (+ or – 2 items).

- **Chunking** (grouping items) can increase the capacity of STM.

- STM is thought to be largely auditory, and items are coded **phonologically**.

- **Rehearsal** (repeating or practicing) is the key to keeping items in the STM and to transferring items to the long-term memory (LTM). **Primary (maintenance) rehearsal** simply involves repeating material in order to hold it in STM. **Secondary (elaborative) rehearsal** involves organizing and understanding material in order to transfer it to LTM.

- STM is susceptible to **interference** (how other information or distractions cause one to forget items in STM). Disrupting information that was learned before the new items were presented, such as a list of similar words, is **proactive interference**. This is problematic for recall and thus causes **proactive inhibition**. Disrupting information that was learned after the new items were presented is called **retroactive interference**. This is also problematic for recall and thus causes **retroactive inhibition**.

Long-Term Memory (LTM)

- Capable of permanent retention.

- Most items are learned semantically, for meaning.

- Long-term memory retention is measured by recognition, recall, and savings.

  - **Recognition** simply requires subjects to recognize things learned in the past. Multiple-choice tests tap recognition.

  - **Recall** requires that subjects generate information on their own. **Cued recall** begins the task; as in fill-in-the-blank tests are an example. **Free recall** is remembering with no cue.

  - **Savings** measures how much information about a subject remains in LTM by assessing how long it takes to learn something the second time as opposed to the first time.

- LTM is subject to the **encoding specificity principle**, which means that material is more likely to be remembered if it is retrieved in the same context in which it was stored.

- LTM is not subject to primacy and recency effects (see p. 39) but is subject to the same interference effects as STM.

EPISODIC VERSUS SEMANTIC MEMORY

- **Episodic memory** consists of details, events, and discrete knowledge.
- **Semantic memory** consists of general knowledge of the world.

PROCEDURAL VERSUS DECLARATIVE MEMORY

- **Procedural memory** is knowing "how to" do something.
- **Declarative memory** is knowing a fact.

BIG WIGS

- **Hermann Ebbinghaus** was the first to study memory systematically. He presented subjects with lists of nonsense syllables to study the STM. He also proposed a **forgetting curve** that depicts a sharp drop in savings immediately after learning and then levels off, with a slight downward trend.

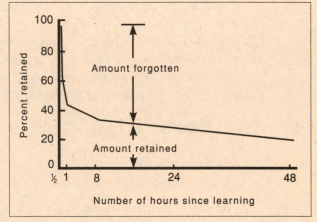

- **Frederick Bartlett** found that memory is **reconstructive** rather than rote. Using the story "War of the Ghosts," he discovered that people are more likely to remember the ideas or semantics of a story rather than the details or grammar of a story.

- **Allan Paivio** suggested with the **Dual Code Hypothesis,** which states that items will be better remembered if they are encoded both visually (with icons or imagery) and semantically (with understanding).

- **Fergus Craik** and **Robert Lockhart** asserted that learning and recall depend on the **depth of processing**. Different levels of processing exist from the most superficial phonological (pronunciation) level to the deep semantic (meaning) level. The deeper an item is processed, the easier it is to learn and recall.

- **Behaviorists** explain memory through **paired-associate learning**. One item is learned with, and then cues the recall of, another.

- **Elizabeth Loftus** found that memory of traumatic events is altered by the event itself and by the way that questions about the event are phrased. "How fast were the cars going when they crashed?" will elicit higher speed estimates than "What was the rate of the cars upon impact?" This finding is particularly important for law-psychology issues, such as the questioning of witnesses.

- **Karl Lashley** found that memories are stored diffusely in the brain.

- **Donald Hebb** posited that memory involves changes of **synapses and neural pathways,** making a "memory tree." **E. R. Kandel** had similar ideas from studying the sea slug Aplysia (see Comparative Psychology). Also, brain studies of young chicks show that their brains are altered with learning and memory.

- **Brenda Milner** wrote about patient "HM" who was given a lesion of the **hippo-campus** to treat severe epilepsy. He could not add anything to his LTM.

OTHER THINGS YOU SHOULD KNOW

- Types of verbal learning and memory tasks:

  - **Serial learning.** A list—such as the presidents of the United States, is learned and recalled in order (**serial recall**). This type of learning is subject to **primacy** and **recency effects**—how the first and last few items learned are easiest to remember, whereas the ones in the middle are often forgotten. First items are remembered because they benefit from the most rehearsal/exposure; last items are easy to remember because there has been less time for decay. The **serial-position curve** (a U-shaped curve on a graph) shows this savings effect.

  - **Serial-anticipation learning.** A list is learned.

  - **Paired-associate learning.** We use this type of learning when we study foreign languages. For example, when studying Spanish, we remember that "coche" means car and "hombre" means man. We pair the Spanish word with the English word.

  - **Free-recall learning.** A list of items is learned, and then must be recalled in any order with no cue.

- The following factors make items on a list easier to learn and retrieve:

  - **Acoustic dissimilarity**

  - **Semantic dissimilarity**

  - **Brevity** (both in the length of the term and in the length of the list of terms to be remembered)

  - **Familiarity**

  - **Concreteness**

  - **Meaning**

  - **Importance to the subject**

- Two main theories suggest the origin of forgetting: decay theory and interference theory. **Decay Theory** (also known as **Trace Theory**) posits that memories fade with time. This theory has been called too simplistic because other activities are known to interfere with retrieval. **Interference Theory** suggests that competing information blocks retrieval. If, for example, two groups learned a list of words, and then one group sleeps while the other group solves riddles, the group that slept is more likely to remember more from the word list. For both groups, the passage of time was the same, but for the riddle group, competing information existed.

- **Mnemonics** are memory cues that help learning and recall. For example, the word "ocean" can be used as a mnemonic to help you remember the Big Five factors of personality: openness, conscientiousness, extraversion, agreeableness, neuroticism.

- The **generation-recognition model** suggests that anything one might recall should easily be recognized. This is why a multiple-choice (or recognition) test is easier than an essay (or recall) test.

- The **tip-of-the-tongue phenomenon** is being on the verge of retrieval but not successfully doing so.

- **State-dependent memory** is like state-dependent learning. Retrieval is more successful if it occurs in the same emotional state or physical state in which encoding occurred. This explains why depressed individuals cannot easily recall happy memories and why alcoholics often remember details of their last drinking session only when under the influence of alcohol.

- **Clustering** is the brain's tendency to group together similar items in memory whether they are learned together or not. Most often, they are grouped into conceptual or semantic hierarchies.

- In a recall task involving the **order of items on a list**, subjects can more quickly state the order of two items that are far apart on the list than two items that are close together. For example, in a list of numbers, subjects can recognize that 7 occurs before 593 more quickly than they can recognize that 133 occurs before 136.

- **Incidental learning** is measured through presenting subjects with items they are not supposed to try to memorize and then testing for learning.

- **Eidetic imagery** is photographic memory. This is more common in children and rural cultures.

- **Flashbulb memories** are recollections that seem burned into the brain, such as "What is your memory of the World Trade Center collapsing?" or "Where were you when you found out John F. Kennedy, Jr. was dead?"

- A **tachtiscope** is an instrument often used in cognitive or memory experiments. It presents visual material (words or images) to subjects for a fraction of a second.

- The **Zeigarnik effect** is the tendency to recall uncompleted tasks better than completed ones.

Study Tip: According to what we know about levels of processing, elaborative rehearsal, and dual code hypothesis, test material will be better retained if you take time to truly understand it. Rote memorization depends only on one link in memory and, is therefore highly susceptible to decay.

6

Cognition

DEFINED: Cognitive psychology is the study of thinking, processing, and reasoning.

PROBLEM SOLVING

- **Concepts** are how one represents the relationship between two things. We organize our world through concepts. "A bird is an animal that has wings and flies."

- **Hypotheses** are ideas used to test relationships and then to form concepts. "Animals with wings are the ones that fly."

- **Mental set** or **set** is the preconceived notion of how to look at a problem. This may help future problem solving. "A bird cage is good for housing birds."

- **Schema** is the cognitive structure that includes ideas about events or objects and the attributes that accompany them. New events and objects are categorized based on how well they match with existing attributes. "This animal has wings, so it is probably a bird."

- **Scripts** are ideas about the way events typically unfold. "When people go to the movies, they sit in their seats and are quiet."

- **Prototypes** are the **representative** or "usual" type of an event or object. "A scientist is someone who is good in math and does not write poetry."

- **Insight** is having a new perspective on an old problem. The A-ha! experience.

- **Convergent thinking** is the type of thinking used to find the one solution to a problem. Math is an example. Convergent and divergent thinking were first defined by **J. P. Guilford**.

- **Divergent thinking** is used when more than one possibility exists in a situation. Playing chess or creative thinking are examples. In a group, the presence of a dissenter leads to divergent thinking.

- **Functional fixedness** is the idea that people develop closed minds about the functions of certain objects. From this, they cannot think of creative uses or think divergently. "A bird cage is only good for housing birds."

- **Problem space** is the sum total of possible moves that one might make in order to solve a problem.

- **Algorithms** are problem-solving strategies that consider every possible solution and eventually hit on the correct solution. This may take a great deal of time.

- **Heuristics** are problem-solving strategies that use rules of thumb or short cuts based on what has worked in the past. A heuristic cannot guarantee a solution but is faster than an algorithm.

- **Metacognition** refers to the process of thinking about your own thinking. It might involve knowing what solving strategies to apply and when to apply them, or knowing how to adapt your thinking to new situations.

- **Mediation** is the intervening mental process that occurs between stimulus and response. It reminds us what to do or how to respond based on ideas or past learning.

- **Computer simulation models** are designed to solve problems as humans do. **Allen Newell** and **Herbert Simon** introduced the first of these (called the **Logic Theorist**) and then revamped it (the **General Problem Solver**).

- **Deductive reasoning** leads to a specific conclusion that must follow from the information given. "All coats are blue. She wears a coat. Therefore, her coat must be blue."

- **Inductive reasoning** leads to general rules that are inferred from specifics. "Most of the Ph.D. students I know studied hard for their GRE. Therefore, studying hard probably helps one do well on the test and then get into school."

- **Logical reasoning errors:**

  - **Atmosphere effect.** When a conclusion is influenced by the way information is phrased.

  - **Semantic effect.** Believing in conclusions because of what you know or think to be correct rather than what logically follows from the information given.

  - **Confirmation bias.** Remembering and using information that confirms what you already think.

INFORMATION PROCESSING

- **Reaction time** is most frequently used to measure cognitive processing. This is also called **latency**. Response speed for all types of tasks declines significantly with age.

- **Elizabeth Loftus** and **Allan Collins** suggested that people have hierarchical semantic networks in their memory that group together related items. The more closely related two items are, the more closely they are located in the hierarchy, and the more quickly a subject can link them. For example, subjects can answer "true" more quickly to the sentence "A canary is a bird" than they can answer "false" to the sentence "A toaster is a bird."

- **Allan Collins** and **Ross Quillian** assert that people make decisions about the relationship between items by searching their cognitive semantic hierarchies. The farther apart in the hierarchy, the longer it will take to see a connection.

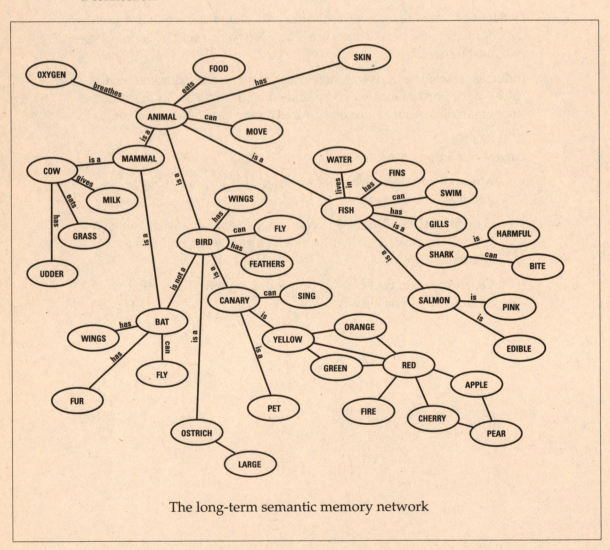

The long-term semantic memory network

- It takes longer to make associations between pictures than between words, probably because pictures must mentally be put into words before associations can be made.

- **Semantic priming** in a word recognition task is the presentation of a related item (such as "test") before the next item (such as "GRE"). Semantic priming decreases reaction time because it activates the node of the second item in the semantic hierarchy. In contrast, it would take longer for subjects to recognize the acronym "GRE" if it were preceded by the word "lobster" rather than by the word "test."

- **Stroop effect** explains the decreased speed of naming the color of ink used to print words when the color of ink and the word itself are of different colors, such as when the word "yellow" is printed with blue ink.

- **Bottom-up processing** is recognizing an item or pattern from data or details (**data driven**). This is opposed to **top-down processing,** which is guided by larger concepts.

- **Automatic processing** is when a task is effortlessly done because the task is subsumed under a higher organization process.

- **Eye movements** and **gaze durations** are indicators of information processing while reading. Eye movements from one fixation point to another are called **saccades**.

COGNITION AND EMOTION

Various theories address the biological and cognitive components of emotion:

- The **James-Lange Theory of Emotion** claims that bodily reactions to situations cause emotion. First, physiological responses are present in situations (crying, fleeing, trembling); then we feel the emotion that comes with these bodily reactions. We feel scared because we are trembling.

- The **Cannon-Bard Theory of Emotion**, also known as the **Emergency Theory**, asserts that emotions and bodily reactions occur simultaneously. In emotional situations, our body is cued to react in the brain (emotion) and in the body (biological response). We tremble and feel scared in response to danger.

- **Stanley Schachter** and **Jerome Singer** proposed a **Cognitive Theory of Emotion**. Similar to the James-Lange Theory, the **Schachter-Singer Theory** asserts that emotions are the product of physiological reactions. But, Schachter and Singer claim that cognitions are the missing link in the chain. A particular bodily state is felt. Since many different situations produce similar bodily reactions, how we interpret the state is key. The cognition we attach to a situation determines which emotion we feel in response to physiological arousal. For example, when a situation causes us to tremble, we feel fear or anger depending on the ideas we have about what emotion fits the situation.

Study Tip: Slow down on EXCEPT/LEAST/NOT questions. It takes longer to process the negative versions or denials of statements. Put a big circle around the entire EXCEPT/LEAST/NOT question and its answer choices. Some students forget that they're dealing with an EXCEPT question by the time they get to choice E. Slow down and be careful.

7

Perception

DEFINED: Perception is how we organize or experience what our sensory systems pick up. Obviously, we sense many more things than we process each second. Also, other factors come to bear on how we understand the sensory information that we receive.

THE BASICS

Different theories exist about the workings of perception:

- **Nativist theory** asserts that perception and cognition are largely innate.

- **Structuralist theory** asserts that perception is the sum total of sensory input. The world is understood through **bottom-up processing.**

- **Gestalt psychology** revolves around **perception** and asserts that people tend to see the world as comprised of organized wholes. The world is understood through **top-down processing.**

- Current thinking, not surprisingly, is that perception is partially innate/sensory, and partially learned/conceptual.

- **Perceptual development** has been explained by **James Gibson** as the increasing ability of a child to make finer discriminations among stimuli. The **optic array**, or all of the things a person sees, trains people to perceive.

VISUAL PERCEPTION

- The **visual field** refers to the entire span that can be perceived or detected by the eye at a given moment.

- The **figure and ground relationship** refers to the relationship between the meaningful part of a picture (the figure) and the background (the ground).

- **Depth perception** has monocular and binocular cues:

  - **Binocular disparity** has been called the most important depth cue. Our eyes view objects from two slightly different angles, which allows us to create a three-dimensional picture.

  - **Apparent size** gives us clues about how far away an object is if we know about how big the object should be.

  - **Interposition** or overlap of objects shows which objects are closer.

  - **Linear perspective** is gained by features we are familiar with, such as two seemingly parallel lines that converge with distance.

  - **Texture gradient** refers to how we see texture or fine detail differently from different distances.

  - **Motion parallax** is how movement is perceived through the displacement of objects over time, and how this motion takes place at seemingly different paces for nearby or faraway objects. Ships far away seem to move slower than nearby ships moving at the same speed.

- **Eleanor Gibson** and **Richard Walk** developed the **visual cliff** apparatus to study whether depth perception is innate. The visual cliff was a thick layer of glass above a surface that dropped off sharply. The glass provided solid, level ground for subjects to move across in spite of the cliff below. Animals and babies were used as subjects, and both groups avoided moving into the "cliff" area regardless of the glass.

Gibson and Walk's visual cliff
(A) originated as market testing for glass-bottom boat excursions
(B) provided valuable information about depth perception in infants

Answer: (B)

- **Afterimages**, also known as the **McCollough Effect**, are perceived because of **fatigued receptors**. Because our eyes have a partially oppositional system for seeing colors, such as red-green or black-white receptors, once one side is overstimulated and fatigued, it can no longer respond and is overshadowed by its opposite. This explains why you see a dark afterimage after staring at a white light.

- **Dark adaptation** is the result of regeneration of retinal pigment.

- **Mental set** factors into why we see what we expect to see.

- **Pragnanz** is the overarching **Gestalt** idea that experience will be organized as meaningful, symmetrical, and simple whenever possible. The following are specific Gestalt ideas:

  - **Closure** is the tendency to complete incomplete figures.

  - **Proximity** is the tendency to group together items that are near each other.

  - **Continuation**, or **good continuation**, is the tendency to create a whole or detailed figures based on our expectations rather than what is seen.

  - **Symmetry** is the tendency to make figures out of symmetrical images.

  - **Constancy** is how people perceive objects in the way that they are familiar with them, regardless of changes in the actual retinal image. A book, for example, is perceived as rectangular in shape no matter what angle it is seen from. **Size constancy** is knowing that an elephant, for example, is large no matter how it might appear. **Color constancy** is knowing the color of an object even with tinted glasses on, for example.

  - **Minimum principle** is the tendency to see what is easiest or logical to see.

- **Classic illusions:**

  - **Ambiguous figures** can be perceived as two different things depending on how you look at them.

  - **Figure-ground reversal patterns** are ambiguous figures, such as the Rubin vase. They can be perceived as two different things depending on which part you see as the figure and which part you see as the background.

  - **Impossible objects** are objects that have been drawn and can be perceived but are geometrically impossible.

  - **Moon illusion** shows how context affects perception. The moon looks larger when we see it on the horizon than when we see it in the sky. This is because the horizon contains visual cues that make the moon seem more distant than the overhead sky. In the overhead sky, we cannot correct for distance when we perceive the size of the moon because we have no cues to work with.

  - **Phi phenomenon** is the tendency to perceive smooth motion. This explains why motion is inferred when there actually is none, often by the use of flashing lights or rapidly shown still-frame pictures, such as in the perception of cartoons. This is **apparent motion**.

Fig. 4 Ambiguous objects a. Duck-rabbit. b. Vasefaces

Two "impossible objects"

- **Müller-Lyer Illusion** is the most famous of all visual illusions. Two horizontal lines of equal length appear unequal because of the orientation of the arrow marks at the end. Inward facing arrowheads make a line appear shorter than another line of the same length with outward facing arrowheads.

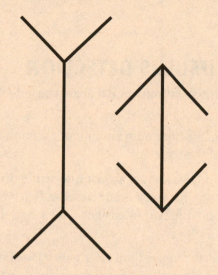

- **Ponzo Illusion** is when two horizontal lines of equal length appear unequal because of two vertical lines that slant inward.

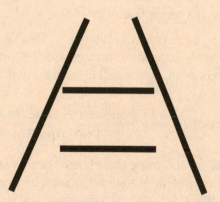

- **Autokinetic effect** is the way that a single point of light viewed in darkness will appear to shake or move. The reason for this is the constant movements of our own eyes.

- **Purkinje Shift** is the way that perceived color brightness changes with the level of illumination in the room. With lower levels of illumination, the extremes of the color spectrum (especially red) are seen as less bright.

- **Pattern recognition** is most often explained by **template matching** and **feature detection**. In order to pick the letter "o" out of a page of letters, we would probably first concentrate only on letters with rounded edges and then look for one to match a typical "o."

- **Robert Fantz** found that infants prefer relatively complex and sensical displays.

THRESHOLD AND STIMULUS DETECTION

Threshold addresses minimum levels of stimulation that are needed for detection. Important types of threshold are as follows:

- **Absolute threshold** is the minimum amount of a stimuli that can be detected 50 percent of the time.

- **Differential threshold** (also known as **just noticeable difference** or **jnd**) is the minimum difference that must occur between two stimuli, so that they are perceived as having different intensities. This was defined by **E.H. Weber**.

- **Terminal threshold** is the upper limit after which the stimuli can no longer be perceived. For example, the lowest pitch sound a human can hear is the absolute threshold, whereas the highest pitch sound a human can hear is the terminal threshold.

Psychophysical explanations for perception of intensity:

- **Weber's Law** applies to all senses but only to a limited range of intensities. The law states that a stimulus needs to be increased by a constant fraction of its original value in order to be noticed as noticeably different. This formula is shown as:

$$\textbf{K (the constant fraction)} = \frac{\Delta \textbf{ I (increase in intensity needed for jnd)}}{\textbf{I (original intensity)}}$$

- **Fechner's Law** is built on, and more complicated than, Weber's Law. In general, it says that the strength of a stimulus must be significantly increased to produce a slight difference in sensation. The law is written as **S (sensation strength) = k log R (a logarithm of the original intensity)**.

J. A. Swet's Theory of Signal Detection (TSD) suggests that subjects detect stimuli not only because they can but also because they want to. TSD factors motivation into the picture, which changes the idea of purely mathematical equations and explains why subjects respond inconsistently. Individuals are partly motivated by rewards and costs in detection. This is **response bias**. The interplay between response bias and stimulus intensity determines responses:

- **False alarms** is saying that you detect a stimulus that is not there.

- A **hit** is correctly sensing a stimulus.

- A **miss** is failing to detect a present stimulus.

- A **correct rejection** is rightly stating that no stimulus exists.

- **Receiver operating characteristic (ROC)** curves are graphical representations of a subject's sensitivity to a stimulus.

OTHER THINGS YOU SHOULD KNOW

- **Simulations** use perceptual cues to make artificial situations seem real.

- **Dichotic presentation** is often used in studies of auditory perception and **selective attention**. In these tasks, a subject is presented with a different verbal message in each ear. Often subjects are asked to **shadow**, or repeat, one of the messages to ensure that the other message is not consciously attended to.

- **Subliminal perception** is perceiving a stimulus that one is not consciously aware of, such as the unattended message in dichotic presentation or visual information that is briefly presented.

> **Study Tip:** Certain subjects might be particularly difficult to retain. Tack a list of researchers or definitions that you are having problems with to your refrigerator or to your mirror. Glancing at them briefly but frequently will eventually cement them in your mind. Afterwards, replace this list with another one.

8

Ethology

DEFINED: Ethology is the study of animal behaviors, especially innate behaviors that occur in a natural habitat.

BIG WIGS

- **Charles Darwin** made the concept of evolution scientifically plausible by asserting that **natural selection** was at its core. For this reason, the concept of evolution is most commonly attributed to him, although he was not actually the first to think of it. His ideas about evolution have been applied to and tested in ethology.

- **Konrad Lorenz, Nikolaas Tinbergen,** and **Karl von Frisch,** all major figures in ethology, shared the Nobel Prize in 1973.

- **Konrad Lorenz** was the **founder of ethology** as a distinct research area. He also created well-known terminology and theory in the field. A question about Lorenz appears on virtually every GRE Psychology Test. Other questions about the areas that he pioneered also show up often. Lorenz is best known for work with:

  - **Imprinting.** Through extensive work with animal social relationships, Lorenz discovered the phenomenon of imprinting. He found that in certain species (most often birds) the young attach to or imprint on the first moving object they see after birth. This attachment is most commonly displayed by a "following response" in which the young chicks will follow their first contact, whether it be an adult bird or an adult human. Lorenz also found that imprinting was subject to a sensitive learning period, after which imprinting would not occur.

© Nina Leen, Life Magazine, Time, Inc.

Lorenz and three of his adopted children.

- **Animal aggression.** Lorenz's theory of instinct fueled the fire of ethology's great debate over innate behavior. Most notably, drawing from Darwin's ideas of natural selection, Lorenz argued that certain kinds of aggression were necessary for the survival of species. Contrary to most psychologists, Lorenz argued that aggressive behavior is instinctual rather than learned and that even human intraspecies aggression can be explained through survival needs.

- **Releasing stimuli.** Lorenz did the earliest work with **releasing stimuli** (also known as **releasers** or **sign stimuli**), which was later continued by Tinbergen. A releasing stimulus in one individual of a species elicits an automatic, instinctual chain of behaviors from another individual in the same species. Lorenz called these elicited chains of behaviors fixed action patterns.

- **Fixed action patterns.** As conceived by Lorenz, fixed action patterns are instinctual, complex chains of behavior triggered by releasing stimuli. They have four defining characteristics: they are **uniform** patterns, they are **performed by most members** of the species, they are more **complex** than simple reflexes, and they **cannot be interrupted** or stopped in the middle. A question about fixed action patterns appears on nearly every GRE Psychology Test.

- **Nikolaas Tinbergen** was one of the founders of modern ethology. Tinbergen is best known for his use of models in naturalistic settings. He continued Lorenz's work with releasing stimuli. Tinbergen's most famous experiments involved stickleback fish and herring gull chicks.

  - In the spring, male **stickleback fish** develop red coloration on their belly, and they fight each other. Tinbergen hypothesized that the **red belly** acted as the releasing stimulus for the attacks. To test this, he built various models of stickleback fish, ranging from very crude models (on which the only feature was a red belly) to very detailed models (which lacked only the red belly). The stickleback males attacked the red-bellied models rather than the detailed but non-red models, thus indicating that the red belly was indeed the sign stimulus for fighting.

  - Hungry **herring gull chicks** peck at the end of their parents' bills, which have a red spot on the tip. The parent then regurgitates food for the chicks. Tinbergen hypothesized that the **red spot on the bill** is what signals the chick to peck at this particular spot. In testing this, he found that chicks pecked more at a red-tipped model bill than at a plain model bill. Further, he found that the greater the contrast between the bill and the red spot, the more vigorously the chicks would peck, even when the contrast was so strong as to be unnatural. This is the concept of the **supernormal sign stimulus**. Supernormal sign stimuli are artificial stimuli that exaggerate the naturally occurring sign stimulus or releaser. They are more effective than the natural releaser.

- **Karl von Frisch** was a major figure in the study of animal behavior. He is most famous for the discovery that honeybees communicate through a dance that they perform (see Comparative Psychology). Von Frisch also studied the senses of fish.

- **Walter Cannon** coined the term **fight or flight**, referring to the change of an animal's internal state in an emergency situation that triggers the animal to choose fight or flight in response. He also coined the term and proposed the idea of **homeostasis**, which is basically the regulation of the body to maintain equilibrium. For example, we perspire when we are too hot and sleep when we are tired.

GENETICS

Genetics questions on the GRE Psychology Test mostly pertain to heredity in humans. **Genes** are the basic unit of heredity. Genes are composed of DNA molecules and are organized in chromosomes. The nucleus of human cells contains 23 *pairs* of chromosomes. Chromosomes in cells act as carriers for genes, and therefore for heredity.

A **gamete**, sperm or ovum in humans, is **haploid** and so contains 23 *single* chromosomes. (All other human cells are **diploid** and contain 23 *pairs* of chromosomes.) The individual of any species is the result of equal genetic contributions from the gamete of two individual parents. The genetic material of one parent neither mixes with nor contaminates the genetic material of the other; rather, two separate sets of 23 chromosomes come together in the **zygote** (the fertilized egg cell) to form 23 chromosome *pairs*. Zygotes are **diploid** because they contain 23 pairs of chromosomes.

The total of all genetic material that an offspring receives (the 23 pairs or 46 total chromosomes) is called the **genotype**. The genotype is an individual's complete genetic makeup, including both **dominant** and **recessive** genes. These possible dominant and recessive gene variations for each characteristic pair up into **alleles**. The two genes that make up the allele occupy the same place on the chromosome. A pair will be constructed as dominant-dominant, recessive-recessive, or dominant-recessive.

Dominant genes always beat out recessive genes. A recessive gene is not manifested unless it is paired with another recessive gene. An individual's combination of dominant and recessive genes determines what he or she looks like on the outside. These external characteristics (eye color, size, etc.) make up the **phenotype**. Phenotypic expression (how one looks and sometimes acts) is partially determined by heredity or genotype, but can also be influenced by the environment.

EVOLUTION AND NATURAL SELECTION

Darwin asserted that, since there is variation among individuals within one species, and since more animals are born than will survive to maturity, a sort of selection process determines which animals survive and reproduce. Individuals best suited to the environment are most likely to survive, and these individuals will pass on their genes. This process in which only the fit survive is called **natural selection** and is at the heart of evolution. Natural selection explains the evolution or genetic development of various species over time. It also explains the concept of **genetic drift** (how particular genotypes are selected out or eliminated from a population over time).

FITNESS

Fitness relates to natural selection's slogan of survival of the fittest. Fitness is the ability to reproduce and pass on genes. Who are the fittest? The fittest animals are sufficiently well suited to the environment to successfully reproduce. This means they have traits that allow them to offset the dangers of competition and predation. This does not mean, however, that individual animals care only about themselves and their own reproduction. In fact, natural selection favors **inclusive fitness** over individual fitness. Inclusive fitness is the concept that animals will be invested in the survival of not only their own genes but also the genes of their kin (since they are carrying the same genes). This **kin selection** creates inclusive fitness. It also explains why parents protect their young and why individual animals may put themselves at risk by sounding alarm calls to warn their siblings of a predator.

INSTINCTUAL BEHAVIOR VERSUS LEARNED BEHAVIOR

Many studies in animal behavior attempt to differentiate between behaviors that are learned and behaviors that are instinctual. **Instinctual** or **innate** behaviors are:

- Present in all normal members of a species

- Stereotypic in form throughout the members of a species, even when performed for the first time

- Independent of learning or experience

Some behaviors have been found to be innate, others learned. Some experiments have shown that there is an interaction between instinct and learning. For example, rodents reared in isolation still perform instinctual nest-building behaviors but their performance is less efficient and less successful than that of rodents also exposed to learning opportunities. The isolated rodents' nests take longer to build and are of poorer construction.

OTHER THINGS YOU SHOULD KNOW

- **Altruism** is behavior that solely benefits another. While actions of inclusive fitness, such as protecting offspring and siblings are somewhat altruistic, an individual is still aiding in the continuation of its genes through this behavior. Truly altruistic behaviors (those toward non-kin) have somewhat baffled ethologists, because they are incompatible with the idea that individuals do what has the greatest survival value for them. Most likely, altruistic behaviors are similar to a group mentality. Individuals will help others if the benefit outweighs the cost or if they expect to be repaid somehow. In this way, altruism is compatible with natural selection.

- **Biological clocks** are internal rhythms that keep an animal in sync with the environment. **Circadian rhythms** are endogenous rhythms that revolve around a 24-hour time period. Other types of internal clocks include the circannual, lunar, or tidal.

- **Courting** refers to behaviors that precede sexual acts that lead to reproduction. Courting serves the purposes of attracting a mate and of isolating a mate of the same species.

- **Displacement activities** (also known as **irrelevant behaviors**) refer to behaviors that seem out of place, and illogical, and have no particular survival function.

- **Estrus** is the period in which a female of the species is sexually receptive.

- **Inbreeding** is breeding within the same family. Evolutionary controls prevent this. An example of such a mechanism is the facial markings of swans. Swans from the same family have similar markings; swans usually choose mates with dissimilar markings.

- **Mimicry** refers to an evolved form of deception. Some harmless species of snakes, for example, mimic the coloration and patterning of poisonous snakes and escape predation as a result.

- **Instinctual drift** occurs when an animal replaces a trained or forced response with a natural or instinctive response.

- **Pheromones** are chemicals that act as messengers between animals. The exchange of pheromones is thought to be the most primitive form of communication between animals. Pheromones can transmit states such as fear or sexual receptiveness.

- **Reproductive isolating mechanisms** serve to prevent **interbreeding** between two different (but closely related and possibly genetically compatible) species. There are four forms of isolating mechanisms:

  - **Behavioral isolation** is when courtship or display behavior of a particular species allows an individual to identify a mate within its own species—only a member of that species will respond to that particular type of courting.

  - **Geographic isolation** is when different species breed in different areas to prevent confusion or genetic mixing.

  - **Mechanical isolation** is when different species have incompatible genital structures.

  - **Isolation by season** is when potentially compatible species mate during different seasons.

- **Sensitive** or **critical periods in learning** are times when a developing animal is particularly vulnerable to the effects of learning (or to the lack of such learning). For example, certain bird species have a critical period for learning the song of their species. If such birds are reared in isolation during this critical period, they cannot develop a normal song later. Critical periods also factor into imprinting. Some developing animals imprint on the first moving objects they experience. Later, they will follow and attempt to mate with this type of animal no matter what their later experiences are.

- **Sexual dimorphism** refers to the structural differences between the sexes. Sexual dimorphism has arisen through both natural and sexual selections.

- **Sexual selection**, according to Darwin in *The Descent of Man* (1871), is a form of natural selection. In sexual selection, however, it is not the fittest that necessarily win out but rather those with the greatest chance of being chosen as a mate (usually the best fighters, the best courters, and the most attractive individuals).

- **Selective breeding** is contrived breeding. Mates are intentionally paired to increase the chances of producing offspring with particular traits.

Study Tip: If you are having trouble remembering a particular fact, study, or researcher, visualize a scenario that will help you remember it. Create an outlandish picture in your mind of the words and concepts that you are trying to recall.

9

Comparative Psychology

DEFINED: **Comparative psychology is closely related to ethology. Through research studies, different species are compared in order to learn about their similarities and differences.** Psychology draws from animal studies to gain insight into human functioning.

IMPORTANT ANIMAL EXPERIMENTS AND DISCOVERIES

BEES, BIRDS, AND BATS

- **Karl von Frisch** discovered the **dance of the honeybees,** which was only one of several important discoveries about the behavior of honeybees.

    - **Communication.** Honeybees communicate by "dancing." Once a scouting bee has located a promising food source, it returns to the hive and conveys the location of food to the rest of the hive through a series of movements. A **round dance** (dancing in circular motion) indicates food that is extremely nearby. A **waggle dance** (dancing with wiggle-type movements) indicates food that is far away. The longer the dance, the farther the food, and the more vigorous the display, the better the food. Most important, the dance is performed on the vertical sheets of the hive. The angle between a perfectly vertical line and the direction the bee orients when dancing is the same angle as between the sun and the food source. The same type of dance is used to communicate potential nesting sites.

    - **Navigation.** Bees are exemplary navigators. Scouting bees do nothing other than look for food and nesting sites and return with the information. While it is known that bees use landmarks as simple location cues, they are also able to use the sun, polarized light, and magnetic fields as navigational aides.

    - **Hierarchy.** Honeybees form a hierarchy within the hive as only one bee emerges as the queen. Once queen, this bee produces a chemical that suppresses the ovaries in all of the other female bees, so that she is the one reproducer. The **queen bee** is constantly tended to and fed by all of the other bees (the female worker bees), and in the spring, she lays thousands of eggs. As these eggs mature, scouts find a new hive site for the old queen and her workers. When a new queen is ready to emerge in a hive, the old queen and her crew depart for a new site.

    - **Mating.** Very few male bees (**drones**) are produced. They serve only one purpose: to mate with the queen. The same mating areas are used year after year even though no bee survives from one year to the next. No one knows how they know to gather in the nearest mating site.

    - **Flower selection.** Bees can see ultraviolet light, so they see flower coloration in a more complex way than humans do. Von Frisch found that honeybees could see certain markers on flowers (**honeyguides**) that people could not.

- **Navigation** is a broad topic, but certain animals are frequently held to be adept navigators. Some animals use a sort of map-and-compass navigation, with the map being landmarks and the compass being sense of direction from elements like the sun or stars. Other animals have true navigational abilities in which they can point toward their goal with no landmarks and from any position. For example, if captured and moved around the world during migration, some birds arrive at their usual goal anyway (true navigation) whereas others are not able to correct their "compass" for the displacement. **Birds** and **bees** are commonly cited as expert celestial navigators. Different cues may serve as a compass:

  - **Atmospheric pressure.** Pigeons are sensitive to pressure changes in altitude.

  - **Infrasound.** Pigeons can hear extremely low frequency sounds (infrasounds) that humans cannot. These low frequency sounds, emitted by surf for example, travel great distances and may be used as a navigational cue.

  - **Magnetic sense.** Pigeons and bees are thought to have magnetic sensitivity, which allows them to use the earth's magnetic forces as cues.

  - **Sun compass.** Both pigeons and bees are known to use the sun as a compass and to compensate for its daily movements.

  - **Star compass.** Many birds use star patterns and movement for navigation.

  - **Polarized light.** When the sun is obscured by clouds, bees can use polarized light to infer the positioning of the sun.

- **Echolocation** is a most sophisticated type of perception, which generally replaces sight. Marine mammals (like dolphins) use echolocation, but **bats** are probably the most commonly used examples. Bats emit high-frequency bursts of sound and locate nearby objects from the echo that bounces off these objects. Though the description is simple, the accuracy of echolocation is not. Research studies have found that bats with 40 cm wing span can fly through grids of thin nylon string, that bats can discriminate between edible and inedible objects, and that bats can locate and eat small flying insects at the rate of two per second.

- **Owls**, like bats, must navigate at night, but owls do not use echolocation. Rather, their hearing is similar to that of humans. Like humans, they judge direction and distance by comparing the differing intensities and arrival times at the two ears. Owls are better than humans at determining elevation of the source of sound; however, because their ears are asymmetrical (one higher than the other), sound from above or below will reach the different ears at different times and with different intensities.

PRIMATES

- **Wolfgang Köhler** acquired fame by experimenting with **chimpanzees** and **insight** in problem solving. Köhler, a Gestalt psychologist, asserted that by perceiving the whole of the situation, chimps were able to create novel solutions to problems (rather than just solve the problems by trial and error). Köhler ran a series of experiments in which chimps had to use tools (long sticks) or create props (stack boxes) to retrieve rewards. Only through insight could the chimp accomplish this. This moment of insight has been referred to as an **A-ha! Experience**.

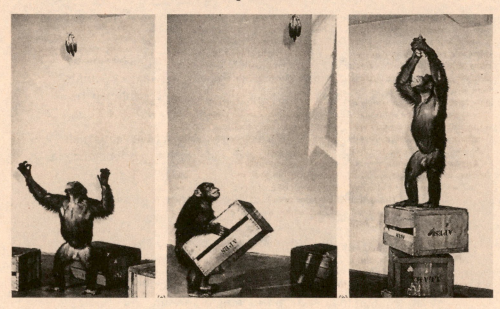

Köhler's chimp Sultan shows off his insight learning.

- **Harry Harlow** researched development with rhesus monkeys. Of particular significance to developmental psychology were his results with social isolation and maternal stimulation.

  - **Social isolation.** Harlow compared monkeys raised in social isolation to monkeys raised with a peer group. With the isolated monkeys, a lack of interaction and socialization with normal, young monkeys hampered their social development. Once brought together with other monkeys, isolated male monkeys did not display normal sexual functioning and isolated female monkeys lacked maternal behaviors.

  - **Contact comfort.** Harlow studied the phenomenon of attachment with infant monkeys. Separated at birth from their mothers, infant monkeys were placed in cages with two "surrogate mothers." One surrogate mother was a plain wire dummy monkey equipped with a feeding bottle and the other surrogate mother was a terrycloth dummy mother with no feeding bottle. Surprisingly, the infant spent most of its time with the terrycloth mother and ran to this surrogate when afraid. The infant approached the wire mother only to feed. It seems then that infants attach to their mothers through comforting experience rather than through feeding.

- **Learning to learn.** Harlow demonstrated that monkeys became better at learning tasks as they acquired different learning experiences. Eventually, monkeys could learn after only one trial. Harlow called this "learning to learn."

OTHER EXPERIMENTS

- **R. C. Tyron** selectively bred "maze bright" and "maze dull" rats to demonstrate the heritability of behavior. Later, **R. M. Cooper** and **John Zubek** demonstrated the interaction between heredity and environment. In the latter experiment, the selectively bred bright rats performed better than the dull rats in maze problem solving only when both sets of rats were raised in normal conditions. Both the bright and dull rats performed well when raised in an enriched environment (with lots of food and available activities, for example); both the bright and dull rats performed poorly when raised in an impoverished environment.

- **Edward Thorndike** acquired fame in animal learning with his concept of **Instrumental Learning**. This type of learning happens through "trial, error, and accidental success." The animal then acts based on previous successes. This led to Thorndike's **Law of Effect**, which postulated that successful behaviors are more likely to be repeated. Thorndike demonstrated the concept with **cats in puzzle boxes**. A cat placed inside the box would eventually accidentally press the escape door lever and be free. In later trials, the cat activates the lever right away (see Learning).

- **Cross fostering experiments** attempt to separate the effects of heredity and environment. If an experiment were to study aggression in rats, it would be difficult to know when genetics influenced aggression or when experience influenced aggression. To correct for this, sibling mice are separated at birth and placed with different parents or in different situations. Later differences in aggression can be attributed to experience rather than genetics.

- **Eric Kandel** studied the **sea slug Aplysia**, which he chose because of its few, large, easily identifiable nerve cells. Kandel posited that learning and memory are evidenced by changes in synapses and neural pathways.

> **Study Tip:** Don't burn out on studying. Though you need a frequent and regular study regimen, taking time off can be important. When you feel really saturated, or the test begins to take on too much of a negative twist, rebel with some time off.

10
Sensation

DEFINED: **Sensation is the feeling that results from physical stimulation.** Sensation involves three steps:

- **Reception** takes place when **receptors** for a particular sense detect a stimulus. The **receptive field** is the part of the world that triggers a particular neuron.

- **Sensory transduction** is the process in which physical sensation is changed into electrical messages that the brain can understand. Sensory transduction is at the heart of the senses.

- The electrical information travels down **neural pathways** to the brain, where the information is understood.

VISION

We see objects because of the light that they reflect. Light is composed of **photons** and **waves** measured by brightness and wavelengths. **Hue** (also known as color) is the dominant wavelength of light. **Brightness** is the physical intensity.

Vision results from the work of many different eye parts:

- The **cornea** is the clear protective coating on the outside of the eye.

- The **lens** is located behind the cornea. **Ciliary muscles** allow it to bend (**accommodate**) in order to focus an image of the outside world onto the retina.

- The **retina**, located on the back of the eye, receives light images from the lens. It is composed of about 132 million of photoreceptor cells and of other cell layers that process information.

- **Receptor cells** (rods and cones) on the retina are responsible for sensory transduction (converting the image into an electrical message the brain can understand). This happens through the chemical alteration of **photopigments**.

- **Rods** are particularly sensitive to dim light and night vision, and they are concentrated along the edges of the retina. This explains why you can see dimly lit objects better with side vision than with forward vision.

- **Cones** are concentrated in the center of the retina (in the area called the fovea). The **fovea** is the area of the retina with the greatest **visual acuity**. Cones are particularly sensitive to color and daylight vision. Cones see better than rods because there are fewer cones per ganglion cell than rods per ganglion cell.

- After light passes through the receptors, it travels through the **horizontal cells** to the **bipolar cells** to the **amacrine cells**. Some information processing probably takes place along the way. Finally, the information heads to the **ganglion cells**, which make up the optic nerves.

- The eyes are connected to the cerebral cortex by a visual pathway. This visual pathway consists of one **optic nerve** connecting each eye to the brain. Along the pathway is an **optic chiasm** in which half of the fibers from the optic nerve of each eye cross over and join the optic nerve from the other eye. Thus, the pathways are 50 percent crossed. This ensures that input from each eye will come together for a full picture in the brain. Because of this layout, a stimulus in the left visual field is processed in the right side of the brain and vice versa. After the optic chiasm, the information travels through the **striate cortex** to the **visual association areas** of the cortex.

Different theories exist for the details of vision:

- **Opponent-color** or **opponent-process** is a theory for color vision proposed by **Ewald Hering**. It suggests that two types of color-sensitive cells exist: cones that respond to blue-yellow colors and cones that respond to red-green. When one color of the pair on a cone is stimulated, the other is inhibited. This is why we don't see reddish-green colors. If an object seems red to us, then our ability to see green in that object is inhibited. This is also why if you look at something red for a long time, and then focus on a white image, you'll see a green **afterimage**.

- The **Tri-Color Theory** was proposed by **Thomas Young** and **Hermann von Helmholtz**. This theory suggests that there are three types of receptors in the retina: cones that respond to red, blue, or green.

- Research shows that the **Opponent-Process Theory** seems to be at work in the lateral geniculate body whereas the **Tri-Color Theory** seems to be at work in the retina.

- **Lateral inhibition** allows the eye to see contrast and prevents repetitive information from being sent to the brain. This complex process is the idea that once one receptor cell is stimulated the others nearby are inhibited.

- **Hermann von Helmholtz** is famous for a theory of **color blindness**.

- **David Hubel** and **Torsten Wiesel** discovered that cells in the visual cortex are so complex and specialized that they respond only to certain types of stimuli. For example, some cells respond only to vertical lines, whereas some respond only to right angles and so on.

HEARING

Humans are sensitive to loudness and pitch in sound.

- The **amplitude** or physical intensity of a sound wave largely determines **loudness**.

- **Frequency**, the pace of vibrations or sound waves per second for a particular sound, determines **pitch**. Low frequency is perceived as low pitch or low tone and vice versa. Frequency is measured in **Hertz (Hz),** and humans best hear frequencies around **1000 Hz**.

- **Timbre** comes from the complexity of the sound wave.

There are three major parts of the ear:

- **Outer ear** consists of the parts that you see called the **pinna** and the **auditory canal**. Vibrations from sound move down this canal to the middle ear.

- **Middle ear** begins with the **tympanic membrane** (also known as the eardrum), which is stretched across the auditory canal. Behind this membrane are the **ossicles** (three small bones), the last of which is the **stapes**. Sound vibrations bump against the tympanic membrane, causing the ossicles to vibrate.

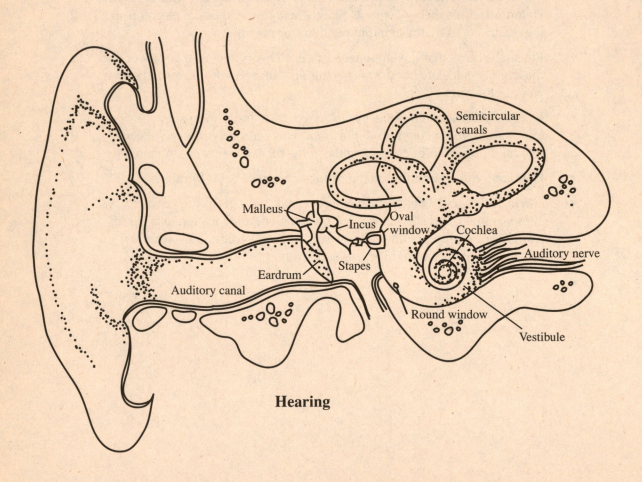

Hearing

- The **inner ear** is responsible for both hearing and balance. It begins with the **oval window**, which is tapped upon by the stapes. These vibrations then activate the fluid-filled, snail-shell-like **cochlea,** which contains the ear parts for hearing (the **basilar membrane** and the **organ of corti**). The movement of the cochlear fluid activates the hair-cell receptors on the basilar membrane and the organ of corti. This movement on the basilar membrane is called the **traveling wave**. The **vestibular sacs** are sensitive to tilt and provide our sense of balance.

- Receptor cells in the inner ear activate nerve cells that change the information into an electrical message the brain can process. The auditory system that leads to the auditory cortex consists of the **olivary nucleus**, the **inferior colliculus**, and the **medial geniculate body**.

Other details:

- **Hermann von Helmholtz** is also famous for the **Place-Resonance Theory** of sound perception, in which different parts of the basilar membrane respond to different frequencies.

- **Sound localization** is achieved in different ways. The degree to which one of our ears hears a sound prior to and more intensely than the other can give us information about the origin of the sound. Specifically, high frequency sounds are localized by intensity differences, whereas low frequency sounds are localized by phase differences.

OLFACTION

Smell is an extremely primitive sense. Hair receptors in the nostrils send their messages to the **olfactory bulb**, which lies at the base of the brain. Smell has been strongly connected to memory and the perception of taste.

GUSTATION

Humans distinguish four basic tastes: **sweet**, **bitter**, **sour**, and **salt**. Most taste receptors lie on the tongue. Saliva mixes with food, so that the flavor can flow easily into the tongue's taste receptors. These taste receptors are called **taste buds** (or **papillae**).

CUTANEOUS/TACTUAL

Human skin senses touch, pain, cold, and warmth.

- **Free nerve endings** in the skin detect pain and temperature changes.

- **Meissner's corpuscles** are receptors in skin that detect touch or contact.

- The size of the **two-point threshold** for touch is largely determined by the density and layout of nerves in the skin.

- **Physiological zero** is the temperature that is sensed as neither warm nor cold.

- **Ronald Melzack and Patrick Wall's Gate Control Theory of Pain** looks at pain as a process rather than just a simple sensation governed in one center in the brain. Melzack and Wall assert that pain perception is related to the interaction of large and small nerve fibers that run to and from the spine. Pain may or may not be perceived depending on different factors, including cognition.

- **Endorphins** are neuromodulators that kick in to reduce or eliminate the perception of pain.

- The **orienting reflex** is the tendency to turn toward an object that has touched you.

OTHER THINGS YOU SHOULD KNOW

- **Kinesthetic sense** or **proprioception** is information from receptors in joints and muscles that tells us about the positioning of our own body.

- **Osmoreceptors** deal with thirst.

> **Study Tip:** Dress appropriately when going to take the GRE Psychology Subject Test. Being too warm causes people to feel sleepy and too relaxed. It's always a good idea to wear layers. Also, rumor has it that wearing a light fragrance enhances attention.

11
Physiological Psychology

DEFINED: **Physiological psychology is the study of the essential biology involved in the study of the mind.** The GRE Psychology Subject Test favors questions about the nervous system, the brain, and neural activity.

THE NERVOUS SYSTEM: BIG PICTURE

- **Central nervous system (CNS).** The CNS is made up of two parts:
  - Brain
  - Spinal cord
- **Peripheral nervous system (PNS).** The pathway that runs to and from the CNS. **Afferent** fibers run toward the CNS, and **efferent** fibers run away from the CNS. The PNS is made up of two parts:
  - **Somatic nervous system** controls voluntary movements of striated muscles.
  - **Autonomic nervous system (ANS)** controls the involuntary physiology of smooth muscles, such as digestion, blood circulation, and breathing. The ANS responds more slowly than the somatic nervous system, which is why we act first in an emergency and then feel the fear. The ANS has two parts:
    - **Sympathetic nervous system** controls arousal mechanisms, such as temperature control, blood circulation, pupil dilation, and threat and fear responses. Lie detector tests rest on the premise that lying activates the sympathetic nervous system.
    - **Parasympathetic nervous system** is responsible for recuperation after arousal.

THE SPINAL CORD

The spine consists of an inner core of **gray matter** (cell bodies and dendrites) and an outer covering of **white matter** (nerve fibers and axon bundles) that go to and from the brain.

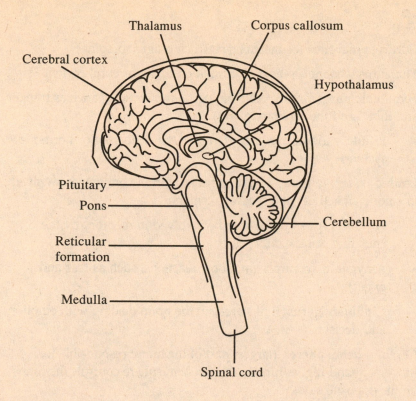

Thalamus

Corpus callosum

Cerebral cortex

Hypothalamus

Pituitary

Pons

Cerebellum

Reticular formation

Medulla

Spinal cord

THE BRAIN

The brain has evolved over time and through species and is an extension of the spine. In general, the brain has developed from the base to the front. You should learn the separate parts of the brain in the general evolutionary order.

- **Hindbrain**

    - **Medulla oblongata** (controls breathing, heartbeat, and blood pressure)

    - **Cerebellum** (controls muscle coordination, balance, posture; its size is related to amount of muscular activity)

    - **Pons** (connects brain parts to spine)

    - **Base of the reticular formation** (considered the **oldest part** of the brain; controls alertness, thirst, sleep, and involuntary muscles such as the heart)

- **Midbrain**

    - **Rest of the reticular formation**

    - **Tectum** (controls vision and hearing)

    - **tegmentum** (controls sleep, arousal, and eye movements)

- Forebrain
  - **Corticospinal tract** (connections between brain and spine)
  - **Thalamus** (channels sensory information to the cerebral cortex)
  - **Hypothalamus** (controls ANS biological motivations, such as hunger and thirst, and the pituitary gland)
    - **Pituitary gland** ("master gland" of the endocrine or hormone system)
  - **Limbic system** (a group of structures around the brainstem involved in emotional activity and pleasure centers)
    - **Hippocampus** (thought to be involved in memory by the encoding of new information)
    - **Amygdala** (controls emotional reactions, such as fear and anger)
    - **Cingulate gyrus** (links areas in the brain dealing with emotion and decisions)
  - **Cerebral hemispheres** (largest part of the brain; responsible for movement and higher functions; each hemisphere controls the limbs on the opposite side)
    - **Corpus collosum** (connects the hemispheres, so they can communicate)
    - **Left hemisphere** (controls speech and motor control)
    - **Right hemisphere** (controls spatial perception and musical ability)
  - **Cerebral cortex** (the outer half-inch of the cerebral hemispheres; the seat of sensory and intellectual functions; split into lobes; also known as the **neocortex**)
    - **Frontal lobe** (controls motor, speech, reasoning, and problem solving; houses Broca's and Wernicke's areas for speech)
    - **Occipital lobe** (responsible for vision)
    - **Parietal lobe** (responsible for somatosensory)
    - **Temporal lobe** (responsible for hearing)
    - **Gyri** (bumps) and **sulci** (fissures) are seen on the cortex surface

OTHER THINGS YOU SHOULD KNOW ABOUT THE BRAIN

- **Meninges** are tough connective tissues covering the brain and spinal cord.

- **Ventricles** are chambers filled with cerebrospinal fluid that insulate the brain from shock.

- **Superior colliculus** (controls visual reflexes) and **inferior colliculus** (controls auditory reflexes) appear as bumps on the brainstem.

- **Basal ganglia** control large muscle movements. Their degeneration is related to motor dysfunction in Parkinson's and Huntington's diseases.

- **Cortical association areas** are areas on the cortex that correspond to certain functions. The larger the area, the more sensitive and highly accessed is the corresponding function. Damage to particular areas would result in certain dysfunction, such as the following:

  - **Apraxia** (inability to organize movement)

  - **Agnosia** (difficulty processing sensory information)

  - **Aphasia** (language disorder; see Broca's and Wernicke's)

  - **Alexia** (inability to read)

  - **Agraphia** (inability to write)

- **Broca's aphasia** is caused by damage to **Broca's area** in the brain. Someone with Broca's aphasia can understand speech but has difficulty speaking (often speaking slowly and laboriously and omitting words).

- **Wernicke's aphasia** is caused by damage to **Wernicke's area** in the brain. Someone with Wernicke's aphasia can speak but no longer understands how to correctly choose words. The person's speech is fluent but nonsensical.

- **Hyperphagia** is overeating with no satiation of hunger. It leads to obesity. Damage to the ventromedial region of the hypothalamus has produced this in animals.

- **Sham rage** is incredible rage easily provoked when the cerebral cortex is removed.

- **Stereotaxic instruments** are used to implant electrodes into animals' brains in experiments.

- Children go through a **blooming and pruning** process in which neural pathways are connected and then some are allowed to die out.

THE NEURON

The **neuron** is the basic unit of the nervous system and has various parts:

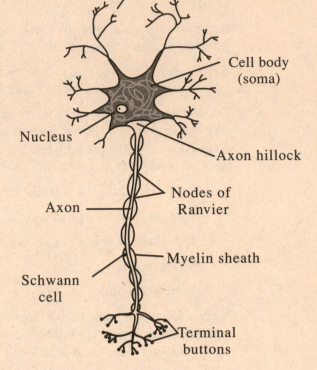

- **Dendrites** are neuron branches that receive impulses. Their branching patterns change throughout life.

- **Cell body**, also known as **soma**, is the largest central portion and makes up **gray matter**. It has a **nucleus** that directs the neuron's activity.

- **Axon hillock** is where the soma and the axon connect.

- **Axon** transmits impulses of the neuron. Bundles of these are nerve fibers, also known as **white matter**. The wider a nerve fiber, the faster its conduction of impulses.

- **Myelin sheath** is a fatty, insulating sheath on some axons that allow faster conduction of axon impulses. It looks like beads on a string.

- **Schwann cell** is the bead-like part of the myelin sheath.

- **Nodes of Ranvier** are the dips between the "beads" on the myelin sheath. They help send the impulse down the axon.

- **Terminal buttons** are the jumping-off points for impulses. They contain **synaptic vessels** that hold **neurotransmitters** (chemicals that stimulate nearby cells).

- **Cell membrane** covers the whole neuron and has selective permeability. Sometimes it lets positive charges (**ions**) through.

- **Synapse**, or **synaptic gap**, is the space between two neurons where they communicate:

  - **Presynaptic cell** is the end of one neuron (the terminal buttons).

  - **Postsynaptic cell** is the beginning of another neuron (the dendrites).

NEURAL TRANSMISSION

Neurons communicate with each other through these steps:

1. **Resting potential** is the inactivated state of a neuron. The neuron is negatively charged at this point, and the cell membrane does not let positive charges (**ions**) in.

2. A **presynaptic cell** fires and releases neurotransmitters from its terminal buttons as a messenger to other neurons.

3. **Postsynaptic receptors** in the **postsynaptic cell** detect the presence of neurotransmitters and cause the ion channels to open.

4. **Postsynaptic potentials** are changes in a nerve cell's charge as the result of stimulation. There are two forms:

    *   **Excitatory postsynaptic potential (EPSP).** In this case, positive charges from the outside are allowed into the cell in a process called **depolarization.** This may cause the nerve to fire.

    *   **Inhibitory postsynaptic potential (IPSP).** In this case, the few positive charges in the cell body are let out, and the cell becomes **hyperpolarized** (or even more negative compared to the outside). This makes the cell even less likely to fire a nerve impulse.

5. **Action potential**, or the **nerve impulse**, begins when a cell becomes stimulated with enough positive ions and "fires."

6. **All-or-none law** refers to the fact that once a minimum threshold for stimulation is met, the nerve impulse will be sent. The intensity of the nerve impulse is always the same, regardless of the amount of stimulation. Intensity of stimulation is indicated by how many signals are fired, not by how strong the signals are.

7. The action potential is sent down the axon, usually by way of the myelin sheath and the nodes of Ranvier. At the terminal buttons, neurotransmitters will be released. Now, this neuron is the presynaptic cell for the next connection.

8. **Absolute refractory period** is the time after a neuron fires in which it cannot respond to stimulation.

9. **Relative refractory period** is the time after the absolute refractory period in which the neuron can fire, but it needs a much stronger stimulus.

10. After a neurotransmitter has done its job, it is either reabsorbed by the presynaptic cell in a process called **reuptake,** or it is deactivated by enzymes. These processes keep the messenger from continually stimulating neurons.

Some important neurotransmitters:

- **Acetylcholine** contracts skeletal muscles.

- **Monoamines** comprise two classes of neurotransmitters:

    - Indolamines, which include **serotonin**. A lack of serotonin is linked to depression.

    - Catecholamines include **dopamine**. Too little dopamine is associated with Parkinson's disease, and too much dopamine is associated with schizophrenia (see Abnormal Psychology).

- Most drugs used in psychology, as well as recreational drugs like cocaine, alter the transmission of neurotransmitters.

- **Neuromodulators** are like neurotransmitters, but they cause long-term changes in the postsynaptic cell.

THE ENDOCRINE SYSTEM

The **pituitary gland**, also known as the master gland, is in charge of the hormone system. The major hormones to know:

- **Androgens** in the bloodstream determine whether an infant mammal will be a male.

- At adolescence, males receive a dose of **androgens,** and females receive a dose of **estrogens**.

- **Follicle-stimulating hormone** and **luteinizing hormone** regulate the development of the sperm and ovum.

- **Prolactin** stimulates milk production.

- **Antidiuretic hormone** causes water retention.

- The **thyroid gland** is triggered by a hormone from the pituitary, the **thyroid-stimulating hormone**.

SLEEP

Electroencephalograms (EEGs) measure brain wave patterns and have made it possible to study waking and sleeping states. Sleep has two distinct components.

- **Non-REM** (Rapid Eye Movement) sleep. Altogether, it takes about a half hour to pass through these four stages of sleep:

  - Stage 0: Prelude to sleep. Low amplitude and fast frequency alpha waves appear in the brain; these waves are also known as **neural synchrony**. A person become relaxed and drowsy and closes the eyes,

  - Stage 1: The eyes begin to roll; alpha waves give way to irregular theta **waves** (lower in amplitude and slower in frequency); the person loses responsiveness to stimuli, experiences, fleeting thoughts

  - Stage 2: The **theta wave** stage, characterized by fast frequency bursts of brain activity called **sleep spindles**, also marked by muscle tension and accompanied by a gradual decline in heart rate, respiration, and temperature.

  - Stage 3: Takes place about 30 minutes after falling asleep. Fewer sleep spindles occur; high amplitude and low frequency **delta waves** appear.

  - Stage 4: Delta waves occur more than 50 percent of the time. These delta waves demarcate the **deepest levels of sleep**, when heart rate, respiration, temperature, and blood flow to the brain are reduced and growth hormones are secreted. A person roused from Stage 4 sleep will be groggy and confused.

- **REM** (Rapid Eye Movement) sleep:

  - Approximately 20 percent of sleep time is spent in REM.

  - REM is interspersed with Non-REM sleep every 30 to 40 minutes throughout the night.

  - REM sleep is when dreams are experienced.

  - REM is characterized by the same fast frequency, low-amplitude beta waves that characterize waking states. Beta waves are also known as **neural desynchrony**.

  - REM sleep is also known as paradoxical sleep. In this state, beta waves and a person's physiological signs—heart rate, breathing, and blood pressure—resemble those in a waking state, but muscle tone decreases to the point of paralysis, with sudden twitches, especially in the face and hands.

  - REM lasts from 15 minutes at the beginning of a sleep cycle to one hour at the end of it.

  - **Rebound effect** occurs when people are deprived of REM sleep. They will compensate by spending more time in REM sleep later in the night.

People complete four to six complete sleep cycles each night. Each cycle lasts about 90 minutes. Early in the night most of the time is spent in Stage 3 and 4 sleep. Stage 2 and REM sleep predominate later on in the night.

- An infant sleeps about 16 hours a day, in contrast to an elderly person who sleeps only about six hours.

- While REM sleep comprises about half of total sleep at birth, it eventually decreases to only 25 percent.

Study Tip: Don't experiment with wonder foods on the day of your GRE Psychology Subject Test. Many health stores sell products that may (or may not) enhance attention and brain power. If you want to try some of these, do it the week before the test. Experiment with what you will eat during the break. Go for a healthy, well-balanced snack. Stay away from sugar, caffeine, or tryptophans (e.g., milk, turkey).

12

Clinical Psychology

DEFINED: Clinical psychology is the study of the theory, assessment, and treatment of mental and emotional disorders. The term "disorder" is used loosely here, referring to anything from life adjustment problems to severe psychopathology. This chapter includes the theories of the major schools of thought, as well as the differing approaches to viewing abnormal behavior and treating clients. Of course, abnormal theory and psychotherapy are complex topics. The GRE Psychology Subject Test only expects you to know the theoretical and technical basics.

PSYCHOANALYTIC THEORY

Originator: **Sigmund Freud**

With psychoanalytic theory, Freud contributed the most extensive and complex theory of human nature. For the subject test, you should know psychoanalytic vocabulary and the history and structure of the theory. Applying the theory is complex and takes years of training. It will not be required of you on the GRE Psychology Subject Test.

Psychoanalytic theory views **conflict** as central to human nature. The conflict is that between different **drives** (particularly conscious and unconscious) vying for expression. The individual is motivated by **drive reduction.** Originally, Freud postulated that an individual's greatest conflict was that between the **libido** (or sexual force) and the **ego**. Later, Freud revised his theory and asserted that the true conflict is that between **Eros** (the life instinct, including sex and love) and **Thanatos** (the death instinct, including self-destructive behavior). This was summed up in Freud's famous quote: "The aim of all life is death."

Another major change in Freud's theory was the way in which he viewed the layout of the mind. Initially, Freud preferred a **topographic** model of mental life in which **conscious** elements were openly acknowledged forces and **unconscious** elements, such as drives and wishes, were many layers below consciousness. Freud's idea of unconscious mental life was perhaps his greatest contribution to psychology. Later, Freud's revised model of mental life was **structural,** meaning that mental life has particular organization other than layers. He organized the mind into three components:

- **Ego.** The part of the mind that mediates between the environment and the pressures of the id and the superego.

- **Id.** The part of the mind that contains the unconscious biological drives and wishes. At birth, mental life is composed solely of the id and its biological drives, such as sex and aggression. With development, the id also includes unconscious wishes.

- **Superego.** The part of the mind that imposes learned or socialized drives. The superego is particularly influenced by moral and parental training.

In psychoanalytic theory, an individual's mental life consists of a constant push-pull between the competing forces of the id, superego, and environment. Each of these areas struggles for acknowledgment and expression. How well a person's ego handles this determines his mental health.

Abnormal theory: Freud often worked with women who were hysterical or neurotic. To Freud, these conditions and other abnormal ones were the result of repressed drives and conflicts, which become manifested in dysfunctional ways. **Pathological behavior, dreams,** and **unconscious behavior** are all symptoms of underlying, unresolved conflict, which are manifested when the ego does not find acceptable ways to express conflict. This is called **psychic determinism.**

Therapy: **Psychoanalysis** or **"analysis"** is a unique form of psychotherapy. A patient in psychoanalysis is usually seen four to five times per week (as opposed to one to two times per week for most other therapies) and often for many years. Portrayals of classic psychoanalysis (as seen in the movie *Harold and Maude*) often include a reclining patient facing away from a very silent analyst. This is an old stereotype; most modern-day analysts run their sessions much like other therapists.

Though initially Freud used **hypnosis** (borrowed from **Jean Charcot** and **Pierre Janet**) with patients, he later switched to the technique of **free association** (developed with **Joeseph Breuer**). Free association is the central process in which a patient reports thoughts without censure or guidance. According to Freud, because unconscious material is always looking for a way out, the patient can uncover and express repressed material through free association. This discharge of repressed emotion is called **catharsis** or **abreaction.**

Another idea central to psychoanalysis is **transference.** Freud postulated that patients would react to the therapist much like they reacted to their parents. The therapist-patient relationship then serves as a metaphor for the patients' repressed emotions about their parents and, thus, as a way of examining those unconscious feelings. **Countertransference** refers to how a therapist feels about his or her patient.

Goal of therapy: Psychoanalysis aims to lessen the unconscious pressures on the individual by making as much of this material conscious as possible. This will allow the ego to be a better mediator of forces.

Criticisms: Freud has been criticized for his methodology. He developed theories from **single case studies** of women in the late 1800s and early 1900s. This is not a "scientific" method (see Research Design).

OTHER VOCABULARY YOU SHOULD KNOW:

- **Aggression.** A central force in humans that must find a socially acceptable outlet.

- **Defense mechanism.** A way in which the ego protects itself from threatening unconscious material or environmental forces. The following are defense mechanisms:

  - **Repression/denial.** Not allowing threatening material into awareness.

  - **Rationalization.** Justifying or rationalizing behavior or feelings that cause guilt.

  - **Projection.** Accusing others of having one's own unacceptable feelings.

  - **Displacement.** Shifting unacceptable feelings or actions to a less threatening recipient.

- **Reaction formation.** Embracing feelings or behaviors opposite to the true threatening feelings that one has.

- **Compensation.** Excelling in one area to make up for shortcomings in another.

- **Sublimation.** Chaneling threatening drives into acceptable outlets.

- **Identification.** Imitating a central figure in one's life, such as a parent.

- **Undoing.** Performing an often ritualistic activity in order to relieve anxiety about unconscious drives.

- **Countertransference.** An analyst's transfer of unconscious feelings or wishes (often about central figures in the analyst's life) onto the patient.

- **Dreams.** Seen as safe outlets for unconscious material and wish-fulfillment. Freud called dreams the "royal road to the unconscious" and saw them as very valuable for analysts. **Manifest content** (the actual content of the dream) provides information about **latent content** (the unconscious forces the dreams are trying to express).

- **The Pleasure Principle.** Also known as **primary process,** this is the human motivation to seek pleasure and avoid pain; it's particularly salient in early life.

- **The Reality Principle.** Also known as **secondary process**. It's guided by the ego and responds to the demands of the environment by delaying gratification.

- **Screen memory.** Memories that serve as representations of important childhood experiences.

INDIVIDUAL THEORY

Originator: **Alfred Adler**

Adler, a colleague of Freud, broke away to create his own theory. In **Individual** or **Adlerian** theory, people are viewed as **creative, social,** and **whole** as opposed to Freud's more negative and structural approach. Adler described people in the process of realizing themselves or in the process of **"becoming."** During this journey, the individual is motivated by **social needs** and feelings of **inferiority** that arise when the current self does not match the self-ideal. A healthy individual pursues goals in spite of feelings of inferiority; a healthy individual has a **"will to power"** or a quest for feelings of superiority. On this quest, a healthy individual will pursue goals that are outside of himself and **beneficial to society**.

Abnormal theory: Unhealthy individuals are too much affected by inferior feelings to pursue the will to power. They may make excuses or have a **"yes, but"** mentality. If they do pursue goals, however, these are likely to be **self-serving** and egotistical.

Therapy: Adlerian therapy is a **psychodynamic** approach in which unconscious feelings do play a role. More importantly, however, is the examination of a person's lifestyle and choices. A patient may examine his motivations, perceptions, goals, and resources.

Goal of therapy: Adlerian therapy aims to **reduce feelings of inferiority** and to **foster social interest** and **social contribution** in patients.

Criticisms: Adlerian therapy is best used with "normal" people in search of growth.

OTHER VOCABULARY YOU SHOULD KNOW:

Adler created a personality typology based on personal activity and social interest:

- **Ruling-dominant type (choleric).** High in activity but low in social contribution; dominant.

- **Getting-leaning type (phlegmatic).** Low in activity and high in social contribution; dependent.

- **Avoiding type (melancholic).** Low in activity and low in social contribution; withdrawn.

- **Socially useful type (sanguine).** High in activity and high in social contribution; healthy.

ANALYTICAL THEORY

Originator: **Carl Gustav Jung**

Carl Jung, Freud's most beloved student, broke from Freud to form his own theory. Jung felt that Freud placed too much emphasis on the libido. Jung's analytical theory postulated that the **psyche** was directed toward **life and awareness** (rather than sex). In each person, the psyche contains conscious and unconscious elements. Most importantly, the unconscious is further divided into two types:

- **Personal unconscious.** Material from an individual's own experiences; this can become conscious.

- **Collective unconscious.** Dynamics of the psyche inherited from ancestors. This is common to all people and contains the archetypes.

The **archetype** is probably Jung's best-known concept. Archetypes are universally meaningful concepts, passed down through the collective unconscious since the beginning of man. Archetypes allow us to organize our experiences with consistent themes and are indicated by cross-cultural similarity in symbols, folklore, and myths. The most commonly cited archetypes are:

- **Persona.** A person's outer mask, the mediator to the external world; this is symbolized in cultures by masks.

- **Shadow.** A person's dark side, often projected onto others; this is symbolized in cultures by devils and evil spirits.

- **Anima.** The female elements that a man possesses; this complements his own maleness.

- **Animus.** The male elements that a female possesses; this complements her own femaleness.

- **Self.** The full individual potential, symbolized in cultures by figures such as Buddha or Jesus; and by the **mandala**.

Abnormal theory: Psychopathology is a signal that something is wrong in the makeup of the psyche. It provides clues about how one could become more aware.

Therapy: The approach is psychodynamic because unconscious elements are addressed. In order to become more aware, unconscious material is explored through the **analysis of an individual's dreams**, artwork, and personal symbols. These are all unconscious messages expressing themselves.

Goal of therapy: Use unconscious messages in order to become more aware and closer to full potential.

Criticisms: Many scientists view Analytic Theory as too mystical or spiritual.

CLIENT-CENTERED THEORY

Originator: **Carl Rogers**
Also known as **person-centered** or **Rogerian** theory, client-centered theory is **humanistic** in that it has an **optimistic** outlook on human nature. Its main tenet is that individuals have an **actualizing tendency** that can direct them out of conflict and toward their full potential. This is best accomplished in an atmosphere that fosters growth.

Abnormal theory: People who **lack congruence** between their real selves and their conscious self-concept develop psychological tension. Incongruence occurs when feelings or experiences are inconsistent with the acknowledged concept of the self. For example, a self-concept that one is perfect will be shaken by experiences of failure.

Therapy: Person-centered therapy is directed by the client, who decides how often to meet and what to discuss in sessions. The therapist is **nondirective**, providing only an atmosphere for the client's self-exploration. The job of the therapist is to provide:

- **Empathy.** The therapist should appreciate rather than just observe the client's world. He or she should attempt to stand in the shoes of the client and take an interest in the client's perspective.

- **Unconditional positive regard.** This facilitates a trusting and safe environment. The therapist maintains positive feelings for the client no matter what choices, feelings, or insights the client explores in therapy.

- **Genuineness/congruence.** The feelings and experiences of the therapist should match, just as those of the client should match. Therapists should not maintain a professional reserve, but instead speak and act genuinely with the client.

Goal of therapy: The aim of client-centered therapy is to **provide a trusting atmosphere** in which the client can engage in self-directed growth and tap his own "vast resources." Evidence of growth includes a **congruent self-concept, positive self-regard,** an **internal locus-of-evaluation,** and **willingness to experience**.

Criticisms: Rogers used no diagnostic tools because he believed that client-centered therapy applied to any psychological problem. Many disagree with this notion.

BEHAVIOR THEORY

Originator: **B. F. Skinner, Ivan Pavlov, Joseph Wolpe**

Behavior theory is the application of classical and operant conditioning principles to human abnormal behavior. It is a model of behavior **based on learning**. Behavioralists change maladaptive behavior through new learning.

Radical behavioralism is associated with **Skinner's** operant ideas that behavior is related only to its consequences. **Neobehavioralism** uses **Pavlov's** classical counter-conditioning principles to create new responses to stimuli.

Abnormal theory: Abnormal behavior is simply the **result of learning**.

Therapy: Behavior therapy is generally **short-term and directed**. Thoughts, feelings, and unconscious motivations are not addressed in behavior therapy. The therapist uses specific **counter-conditioning** techniques to foster the learning of new responses in the client. The most cited techniques are the following:

- **Systematic desensitization,** developed by **Joseph Wolpe**, applies **classical** conditioning in order to **relieve anxiety**. The client is given repeated exposure to the anxiety-producing stimulus in a relaxing situation. The first step is often **imagery** (imagining the stimulus); eventually, the anxiety response will be extinguished.

- **Flooding** or **implosive therapy** applies **classical** conditioning in order to **relieve anxiety**. The client is repeatedly exposed to an anxiety-producing stimulus, so that, eventually, the overexposure simply leads to lessened anxiety.

- **Aversion therapy** employs the **operant** principle of negative reinforcement in order to **increase anxiety**. An anxiety-reaction is created where there previously was none. This is generally used to treat **fetishes.**

- **Shaping** uses **operant** conditioning to change behavior. The client is reinforced for behaviors that come closer and closer to the desired action.

- **Modeling** employs **social learning** principles; this method exposes the client to more adaptive behaviors.

- **Assertiveness training** provides tools and experience through which the client can become more assertive.

- **Role playing** allows a client to practice new behaviors and responses.

Behavioral treatment of phobias

Professor Gallagher and his controversial technique of simultaneously confronting the fear of heights, snakes and the dark.

Goal of therapy: To change behavior in the desired or adaptive direction. Behavior therapy has been extremely successful in treating **phobias, fetishes, obsessive-compulsive disorder, sexual problems,** and **childhood disorders** (particularly nocturnal enuresis or bed-wetting).

Criticisms: Behavior therapy has been accused of **treating the symptoms** rather than the underlying problem.

COGNITIVE THEORY

Originator: **Aaron Beck**

Cognitive theory gives **conscious thought patterns** (as opposed to emotions or behaviors) the starring role in people's lives. Beck posited that thoughts determined feelings and behavior. The way a person interprets experience, rather than the experience itself, that is what's important.

Abnormal theory: **Maladaptive cognitions** lead to abnormal behavior or disturbed affect. Various types of maladaptive cognitions exist:

- **Arbitrary inference.** Drawing a conclusion without solid evidence: "My boss thinks I'm stupid because he never asks me to play golf."

- **Overgeneralization.** Mistaking isolated incidents for the norm: "No one will ever want to be with me."

- **Magnifying/minimizing.** Making too much or little of something: "It was luck that I did well on my exam."

- **Personalizing.** Inappropriately taking responsibility: "Our office's failed project was all my fault."

- **Dichotomous thinking.** Black and white thinking: "If I don't score an 800 on the GRE, I'll have no future."

Beck postulated that a **cognitive triad** (negative views about the self, the world, and the future) causes such depression. The **Beck Depression Inventory** (**BDI**) measures such views and is used to gauge the severity of diagnosed depression.

Therapy: **Directed** therapy helps to expose and restructure maladaptive thought and reasoning patterns. This is generally **short-term** therapy in which the therapist focuses on **tangible evidence of the client's logic** (such as what the client says and does).

Goal of therapy: To correct maladaptive cognitions.

Criticisms: Similar to behavior therapy, cognitive therapy addresses how a person thinks, rather than why the thought patterns were initially developed. **Removing the symptoms** (maladaptive cognitions) may not cure the problem.

RATIONAL-EMOTIVE THEORY

Originator: **Albert Ellis**

Rational-Emotive Theory (RET) includes elements of cognitive, behavioral, and emotion theory. Ellis believed that intertwined thoughts and feelings produce behavior.

Abnormal theory: Psychological tension is created when an **a**ctivating event occurs (**A**), and a client applies certain **b**eliefs about the event (**B**), and this leads to the **c**onsequence of emotional disruption (**C**).

Therapy: Therapy is highly **directive**. The therapist leads the client to dispute (**D**) the previously applied irrational beliefs.

Goal of therapy: The goal is for **e**ffective rational beliefs (**E**) to replace previous self-defeating ones. Then a client's thoughts, feelings, and behaviors can coexist.

Criticisms: Like cognitive and behavior theory, RET has been called **too sterile** and mechanistic.

GESTALT THEORY

Originator: **Fritz Perls**, **Max Wertheimer**, **Kurt Koffka**

Gestalt theory encourages people to stand apart from beliefs, biases, and attitudes derived from the past. The goal is to **fully experience and perceive the present** in order to become a whole and integrated person.

Abnormal theory: Abnormal behavior is derived from **disturbances of awareness**. The client **may not have insight** (the ability to see how all the pieces of experience fit together), or the client **may not fully experience** his present situation (choosing not to acknowledge certain aspects of the situation).

Therapy: The Gestalt therapist engages in a **dialogue** with the client, rather than leading the client toward any particular goal. The client learns from the shared dialogue. Together they focus on the **here and now** experience, rather than talking about the past.

Goal of therapy: The goal is **exploration of awareness and full experiencing of the present**. A successful therapy connects the client and her present existence.

Criticisms: This therapy is not suited for low-functioning or disturbed clients.

EXISTENTIAL THEORY

Originator: **Victor Frankl**

Existential theory revolves around age-old philosophical issues, particularly the issue of meaning. According to existential theory, a person's greatest struggles are those of **being vs. nonbeing** and of **meaningfulness vs. meaninglessness**. An individual is constantly striving to rise above a simple behavioral existence and toward a genuine and meaningful existence. Frankl called this **"will to meaning." Rollo May** is a major contributor to existential therapy.

Abnormal theory: The response to perceived meaninglessness in life is neurosis or **neurotic anxiety** (as opposed to normal or justified anxiety).

Therapy: Existential therapy is talking therapy in which deep questions relating to the client's perception and meaning of existence are discussed.

Goal of therapy: The goal is to increase a client's sense of being and **meaningfulness**. This will alleviate neurotic anxiety.

Criticisms: This therapy has been called too abstract for severely disturbed individuals.

PSYCHOPHARMACOLOGY

Rather than a school of thought, psychopharmacology is the use of medication to treat mental illness. While drugs do not cure mental illness, some are very effective at alleviating symptoms. Sometimes drugs are the only treatment a client needs or receives. In other cases, medication is used in conjunction with therapy.

Abnormal theory: It is believed that some emotional disturbances are at least partly caused by **biological factors** and, therefore, can be successfully treated with medication.

- *Therapy*: Most "psychopharm" treatments aim to affect **neurotransmitters**, which are the natural chemicals in your brain that transmit impulses from one neuron to another across synapses. The most common neurotransmitters acted upon are: **dopamine, serotonin;** and **norepinephrine.** All of these neurotransmitters are in the class of **momoamines**.

- **Antipsychotics.** These were the first drugs used for psychopathology. They were usually used to treat positive symptoms of schizophrenia, such as delusions and hallucinations, by blocking dopamine receptors and inhibiting dopamine production. Examples include: chlorpromazine (Thorazine®) and haloperidol (Haldol®).

- **Antimanics.** Drugs of choice to manage bipolar disorder. They inhibit monoamines such as norepinephrine and serotonin, based on the theory that mania results from excessive monoamines. For example: lithium.

- **Antidepressants.** Used to reduce depressive symptoms by taking the opposite action of antimanics. The theory is that abnormally low levels of monoamines cause depression. These drugs act to increase the production and transmission of various monoamines.

  - **Monoamine oxidase inhibitors (MAOIs).** For example: phenelzine (Nardil®).

  - **Selective serotonin reuptake inhibitors (SSRIs).** Act only on serotonin (hence the name "selective") and so are a great step forward for specific drug effects. For example: fluoxetine (Prozac®), paroxetine (Paxil®), and sertraline (Zoloft®).

  - **Tricyclic antidepressants (TCAs).** Have a tricyclic chemical structure. For example: amitriptyline (Elavil®).

- **Anxiolytics.** Used to reduce anxiety or induce sleep. They also have high potential for causing habituation and addiction. For example: barbiturates and benzodiazepines such as diazepam (Valium®) and alprazolam (Xanax®).

- **Antabuse.** Drug that changes the metabolism of alcohol, resulting in severe nausea and vomiting when combined with alcohol; it can be used to countercondition alcoholics.

Goal of therapy: To provide relief from symptoms of psychopathology.

Criticisms: Drugs that take away symptoms do not provide interpersonal support.

OTHER THINGS YOU SHOULD KNOW

- **Hans Eysenck** criticized the effectiveness of psychotherapy after analyzing studies that indicated psychotherapy was no more successful than no treatment at all. Other studies have since contradicted this point.

- **Anna Freud** applied Freudian ideas to child psychology and development.

- **Melanie Klein** pioneered **object-relations theory** and psychoanalysis with children.

- **Neo-Freudians** accept some of Freud's ideas and reject others:

  - **Karen Horney** emphasized culture and society over instinct. She suggested that neuroticism is expressed as movement toward, against, and away from people.

  - **Harry Stack Sullivan** emphasized social and interpersonal relationships.

- **Psychodynamic theory** is a general term that refers to theories (such as Individual or Analytical) that emphasize the role of the unconscious.

- **Cognitive Behavioral Therapy (CBT)** employs principles from cognitive and behavioral theory.

- **Humanistic theory** is a general term that refers to theories (such as client-centered, Gestalt, or Existential) that emphasize the positive, evolving free will in people. This type of theory is optimistic about human nature. It is also known as the **"Third Force"** in psychotherapy in reaction to psychoanalysis and behavioralism.

- **Abraham Maslow** was the leader of the **humanistic** movement in psychology. Maslow is best known, not for any contribution to therapy, but for his pyramid-like **hierarchy of needs**, which really pertains to human motivation. Maslow asserted that humans start at the bottom and work their way up the hierarchy toward self-actualization by satisfying the needs at the previous level. Here are the levels from top to bottom:

  self-actualization
  esteem and recognition
  belonging, love, acceptance
  safety, security, stability, lack of fear
  physiological needs, hunger, thirst, shelter, warmth

- **Play therapy** is used with child clients. During play, a child client may convey emotions, situations, or disturbances that might otherwise go unexpressed.

- **Electroconvulsive shock therapy (ECT)** delivers electric current to the brain and induces convulsions. It is an effective intervention for severely depressed patients.

- **Family therapy** treats a family together and views the whole family as the client.

- **Stress-inoculation training**, developed by **Donald Meichenbaum**, prepares people for foreseeable stressors.

- **Neil Miller** proved experimentally that abnormal behavior can be learned.

- **Evidence-based treatment** refers to treatment for mental health problems that has been shown to produce results in empirical research studies (for example, studies randomly assigning individuals to types of treatment and following other rules of good research design). Many clinics and researchers argue that only treatment that has been shown to work in research is ethical. Other clinics and researchers argue that controlled experiments are nothing like a real treatment environment and so the results are not as useful (or as widely applicable) as one might suppose.

- In the treatment of depression, anti-depressants are often employed, either because relatively fast relief from symptoms is needed so that the individual can even attend therapy, or because psychotherapy has been unsuccessful. Anti-depressants usually require at least six weeks to begin working.

Study Tip: Use systematic desensitization for your own test stress—imagine the test and imagine it going well. Study in the actual room or building where you will have your GRE Psychology Subject Test. Also, replace black-and-white thinking with realistic but optimistic thinking. Many students think that if they don't get a 750 then they will never have a successful career. These thoughts cause stress and reduce performance. Think positively and realistically!

13

Abnormal Psychology

DEFINED: Abnormal psychology is the study of behavior that is deemed not normal. People who display abnormal behavior may be diagnosed with a particular mental disorder. According to the *Diagnostic and Statistical Manual, fourth edition* (DSM-IV), the American Psychiatric Association diagnostic manual, mental disorders fall into 16 major categories. Probably the best way to understand the relationship between the various disorders is to learn them in the format of the DSM-IV. Below, abnormal behaviors are described in DSM-IV groupings. As some disorders are cited more often than others on the GRE Psychology Test, the descriptions of the disorders vary in length.

DISORDERS OFTEN DIAGNOSED IN CHILDHOOD/ADOLESCENCE

- **Mental Retardation.** Indicated by IQ of 70 or below. Mild = IQ of 55–70, moderate = IQ of 40–55, severe = IQ of 25–40, profound = IQ < 25

- **Learning Disorders.** Indicated by school achievement or standardized scores at least 2 standard deviations below the mean for the appropriate age and IQ.

- **Developmental Disorders.** Autism, for example; indicated by severe problems with social skills, communications, and interests.

- **Attention-Deficit and Disruptive Behavior Disorders**

    - Attention-deficit/hyperactivity disorder (ADHD) is indicated by problems with attention, behavior, and impulsivity.

    - Conduct disorder is indicated by patterns of behavior that violate rules, norms, or the rights of others.

- **Tic Disorders.** Tourette's syndrome, for example, is indicated by motor and vocal tics.

- **Elimination Disorders.** Nocturnal enuresis, for example, is bed-wetting.

DELIRIUM, DEMENTIA, OTHER COGNITIVE DISORDERS

- **Delirium.** Indicated by disturbed consciousness (awareness, attention, focus) and cognition (memory, disorientation).

- **Dementia.** Cognitive problems (with memory, spatial tasks, or language) that result from a medical condition; may be the result of **Alzheimer's, Parkinson's** (tremors with declining neurological functioning), **Huntington's disease** (genetically inherited progressive degeneration of thought, emotion, and movement), or **Pick's disease** (disease of the frontal and temporal lobes of the brain characterized by changes in personality).

MENTAL DISORDERS DUE TO A GENERAL MEDICAL CONDITION

Disorders in this category are the direct physiological result of a medical problem, such as depression resulting from hypothyroidism.

SUBSTANCE-RELATED DISORDERS

These include disorders that result from the use of any toxin such as cocaine, nicotine, or paint fumes. The two best-known subtypes:

- **Dependence.** Indicated by some combination of the following: continued use despite substance-related problems; need for increased amount of substance; a desire but inability to stop use; withdrawal; lessening of outside interests; lots of time spent getting, using, or recovering from the substance.

- **Abuse.** Recurrent use despite substance-related problems or danger.

SCHIZOPHRENIA AND OTHER PSYCHOTIC DISORDERS

Each disorder in this category is a **psychotic** disorder, which means that hallucinations or delusions (erroneous beliefs) are present.

- **Schizophrenia**, formerly known as **dementia praecox**, was renamed by **Eugene Bleuler**. Schizophrenia means "split mind," indicating a mind that has split from reality. Though the community frequently confuses schizophrenia with multiple personality disorder, schizophrenia is *not* the same as multiple personalities or a split personality. For some reason, schizophrenia is a favorite on the GRE Psychology Subject Test.

  Schizophrenic symptoms may be positive (abnormally present) or negative (abnormally absent). Positive symptoms include **delusions** (erroneous or distorted thinking); **perceptual hallucinations**; nonsensical or **disorganized speech** (perhaps use of made up words called **neologisms**); and **disorganized behavior** (inappropriate dress, agitation, shouting). Negative symptoms include **flat affect** (absence of appropriate emotion) or restrictions in thought, speech, or behavior.

  The onset of schizophrenia is generally between late adolescence and the mid-30s. **Process schizophrenia** develops gradually, whereas **reactive schizophrenia** develops suddenly in response to a particular event. Process schizophrenia has a lower rate of recovery than reactive schizophrenia. Generally, an individual with a history of good social and interpersonal skills is more likely to recover from schizophrenia than an antisocial individual.

  The cause of schizophrenia is at least partially physiological. According to the **diathesis-stress theory**, schizophrenia results from a physiological predisposition (abnormal brain chemistry) paired with an external stressor. The biochemical factor most associated with schizophrenia is **excessive dopamine** in the brain.

There are five main types of schizophrenia:

- **Paranoid.** Indicated by preoccupation with delusions or auditory hallucinations.

- **Disorganized.** Also known as **hebephrenic** schizophrenia; indicated by disorganized speech and behavior, and flat affect.

- **Catatonic.** Indicated by the following: psychomotor disturbance, such as **catalepsy** (motor immobility or waxy figure); excessive motor activity; prominent posturing (gestures, mannerisms, or grimacing); **echolalia** (parroting); or **echopraxia** (imitating the gestures of others).

- **Undifferentiated.** A grab bag of schizophrenic symptoms not fitting into a particular type.

- **Residual.** Watered-down schizophrenia with few positive symptoms, if any.

- **Schizoaffective disorder.** Schizophrenic symptoms accompanying a depressive episode.

- **Delusional disorder.** Persistent delusions of various types: **erotomanic** (that another person is in love with the individual); **grandiose** (that one has special talent or status); **jealousy**; **persecutory**; **somatic** (bodily, such as believing a part of the body is ugly or misshapen).

- **Shared psychotic disorder.** Also known as "folie a deux;" when two people have shared delusions.

MOOD DISORDERS

- **Major depressive disorder.** A depressive episode evidenced by depressed mood, loss of usual interests, changes in weight or sleep, low energy, feelings of worthlessness, or thoughts of death; the symptoms are present nearly every day for at least two weeks.

- **Dysthymic disorder.** Symptoms of major depressive disorder are present more days than not for over two years.

- **Bipolar disorder.** Also known as manic depression. It's indicated by depressive symptoms that alternate with manic symptoms (inflated self-esteem, decreased sleep, talkativeness, flight of ideas, intense goal-directed activity, excessive pleasure-seeking).

ANXIETY DISORDERS

One component of many different anxiety disorders is the **panic attack**. Such an attack lasts only for a discrete period of time, often under 10 minutes. During a panic attack, an individual has overwhelming feelings of danger or of the need to escape. This is often expressed as an intense fear of spontaneously dying or "going crazy" and is generally accompanied by physical manifestations such as sweating, trembling, pounding heart, and more.

- **Panic disorder.** Recurrent panic attacks and persistent worry about another attack; this disorder is often accompanied by a mitral valve heart problem.

- **Agoraphobia.** Fear of a situation in which panic symptoms might arise and escape would be difficult; this usually means fear and avoidance of being outside the home or in crowds.

- **Phobia.** Recognized, unreasonable, intense anxiety symptoms and avoidance anchored to a stimulus. **Specific phobia** is anxiety in response to a stimulus, such as flying, heights, needles, or driving; **social phobia** pertains to anxiety around social or performance situations.

- **Obsessive-compulsive disorder.** Characterized by **obsessions** (persistent thoughts) or **compulsions** (repetitive behaviors or mental acts) that are time consuming, distressing, and disruptive. Typical obsessions might be uncontrollable thoughts of worrying about locking the door or about becoming contaminated; typical compulsions might be checking behavior, praying, counting, or hand washing.

- **Posttraumatic Stress Disorder (PTSD).** Exposure to trauma that results in decreased ability to function and recurrent thoughts and anxiety about the trauma; this disorder is often linked to war veterans or victims of violence.

SOMATOFORM DISORDER

These disorders are manifested by physical or bodily symptoms that cause reduced functioning.

- **Conversion disorder.** Psychological problems are converted to bodily symptoms; the symptoms generally relate to voluntary movement and may be manifested as "paralysis" in part of the body. This disorder was formerly known as "hysteria," from Freud's work.

- **Hypochondriasis.** Irrational concern about having a serious disease.

FACTITIOUS DISORDER

Creating physical complaints through fabrication or self-infliction (ingesting toxins, for example) in order to assume the sick role.

DISSOCIATIVE DISORDERS

These disorders all involve the disruption of memory or identity. They were formerly known as **psychogenic disorders**.

- **Amnesia.** Inability to recall information relating to trauma. **Retrograde amnesia** is the forgetting of events that occurred before the trauma; **anterograde amnesia** is the forgetting of events that occurred after the trauma.

- **Fugue.** Suddenly fleeing to a new location, forgetting true identity, and/or establishing a new identity.

- **Identity disorder.** Dissociative identity disorder is the new name for **multiple personality disorder**, or the assumption of two or more identities that control behavior in different situations.

SEXUAL AND GENDER IDENTITY DISORDERS

These disorders range from fetishes to arousal problems to gender discomfort. Anything sexual is under this category.

EATING DISORDERS

- **Anorexia nervosa.** Refusing to eat enough to maintain a healthy body weight; showing excessive concern about becoming obese.

- **Bulimia nervosa.** Binge eating accompanied by harmful ways to prevent weight gain (induced vomiting or laxative use).

SLEEP DISORDERS

Dyssomnias relate to sleep abnormalities. **Parasomnias** are abnormal behaviors during sleep.

- **Insomnia.** Difficulty falling asleep or staying asleep.

- **Hypersomnia.** Excessive sleepiness.

- **Narcolepsy.** Falling asleep uncontrollably during routine daily activity.

- **Nightmare.** Frequent disruption of sleep because of nightmares.

- **Sleep terror.** Frequent disruption of sleep because of screaming or crying.

IMPULSE CONTROL DISORDERS (NOT ELSEWHERE CLASSIFIED)

For each of these, an irresistible urge dictates behavior. Giving in to the impulse usually lessens tension and brings relief, though the behavior is disruptive to overall functioning.

- **Kleptomania.** Irresistible impulse to steal.
- **Pyromania.** Irresistible impulse to set fires.
- **Pathological gambling.** Irresistible impulse to gamble.
- **Trichotillomania.** Irresistible impulse to pull out one's own body hair.

ADJUSTMENT DISORDERS

The presence of a real stressor (a move, a divorce, city life) that results in decreased functioning.

PERSONALITY DISORDERS

These disorders are characterized by rigid, pervasive, culturally abnormal personality structures. There are several types of personality disorders:

- **Paranoid.** Distrust, suspicion.
- **Schizoid.** Detachment, small range of emotion.
- **Schizotypal.** Eccentricity, distorted reality.
- **Antisocial.** Disregard for the rights of others. Absence of guilt.
- **Borderline.** Instability in relationships and emotions, impulsivity.
- **Histrionic.** Excess emotion, attention-seeking.
- **Narcissistic.** Need for admiration, idea of superiority.
- **Avoidant.** Social inhibitions, hypersensitivity perceptions of inadequacy.
- **Dependent.** Need to be taken care of, clinging.
- **Obsessive-compulsive.** Excessive orderliness and control, perfectionism.

OTHER THINGS YOU SHOULD KNOW

- **Dopamine** is a major player in the physiology of various disorders.
  - Too much dopamine activity is believed to cause **schizophrenia**.
  - The use of **amphetamines** increases dopamine activity and, thus, produces schizophrenic-like paranoid symptoms.
  - **Neuroleptic** drugs (such as the antipsychotic chlorpromazine) reduce dopamine activity by blocking dopamine receptors; thereby reducing schizophrenic symptoms.

- Parkinson's is caused by **deficient dopamine activity**. Someone with Parkinson's needs to boost dopamine activity through use of a drug such as levodopa. Neuroleptics can cause Parkinson's because they decrease dopamine activity.

- **Tardive dyskinesia** can also result from the long-term use of neuroleptics or psychotropics. This disorder is characterized by involuntary, repetitive movements of the tongue, jaw, or extremities.

- **Down syndrome** is the most common cause of mental retardation. Down syndrome results from a chromosomal abnormality, namely a trisomy of chromosome 21. In other words, an individual with Down syndrome has three chromosomes, rather than two, on the 21st chromosome. Older mothers having a greater chance of having a baby with Down syndrome.

- **Cretinism** is a different form of mental retardation that is caused by iodine deficiency.

- Two organic disorders result from years of heavy drinking: Korsakoff's syndrome and Wernicke's syndrome.

  - **Korsakoff's syndrome**, caused by vitamin B deficiency, is the loss of memory and orientation. Sufferers often make up events to fill in the gaps. (These are **confabulations.**)

  - **Wernicke's syndrome**, caused by thiamine deficiency, is characterized by memory problems and eye dysfunctions.

- **Phenylketonuria (PKU)** is an infant disease related to excess amino acids. It is an inborn error of metabolism.

- **Tay-Sachs disease** is a genetic deficiency of hexosaminidase A. Sufferers may have symptoms that resemble psychological disorders, such as schizophrenia or dementia.

- A male with two X and one Y chromosomes is said to have **klinefelter's syndrome**.

- **Depression** has a higher occurrence rate in developed countries. Also, women are two times more likely to be diagnosed with unipolar depression than are men.

- **Reactive depression,** or the depression resulting from particular events, has been noted for its similarity to **Martin Seligman's** idea of **learned helplessness**.

- **Thomas Szasz** viewed the schizophrenic world as simply misunderstood or artistic. He felt that schizophrenics should not be treated.

- **Depressive realism:** refers to the finding that depressed people tend to be more realistic about life than the non-depressed.

- **Fromm** and **Reichman** coined the term **schizophrenogenic mother,** which refers to a type of mother who supposedly causes children to become schizophrenic.

- **David Rosenhan** studied the effect of diagnostic labels on the perception of behavior. In an experiment, normal pseudopatients were admitted to hospitals feigning disorders. Once inside, the individuals acted normally, but their behaviors were construed as fitting the diagnosis anyway.

- **Life event stress** most frequently results from large, sudden changes or problems.

Study Tip: Taking the GRE Psychology Subject Test is stressful enough! Don't try to take your tests while changing other large aspects of your life. Tone things down. Keep it simple. Reduce all other stress on the morning of the test, set an alarm and have a good friend call to wake you up, so you don't worry about sleeping through your alarm.

14

Developmental Psychology

DEFINED: **Developmental psychology is the study of changes and transitions that accompany physical growth or maturation.** Tied with Social Psychology as the area with the highest number of questions, Developmental Psychology is quite important on the test. At the very least, know your Piaget!

PHYSIOLOGICAL DEVELOPMENT

In humans, fertilization occurs in the fallopian tube of the female when a sperm unites with an egg or ovum and travels to the uterus. The **zygote** (the fertilized ovum) then goes through three stages of **gestation** or prenatal development:

- The **germinal** stage lasts two weeks, during which time the zygote moves down the fallopian tube, grows into 64 cells through cell division, and implants itself into the wall of the uterus.

- The **embyronic** stage lasts until the end of the second month and consists of genitalia and organ formation.

- The **fetal** stage lasts from the third month until birth. Quantitative growth occurs during this time, as well as movement (called "quickening"). If a fetus has the steroid hormone **androgen** in its bloodstream, it will be male; if it is lacking **androgens**, it will be female.

A **neonate** is a newborn. The behavior of neonates is reflexive. The best known reflexes are the **sucking reflex** (elicited by placing an object in the baby's mouth), **head turning reflex** (elicited by stroking the baby's cheek), **Moro reflex** (the throwing out of arms and legs elicited by loud or frightening noises), **Babinski reflex** (the fanning of the toes elicited by touching the bottom of the baby's foot), and **Palmar reflex** (the hand grasping elicited by placing an object in the baby's hand).

The other most commonly addressed developmental stage is **adolescence**. This period spans the teen years (13 to 19) and begins with the onset of puberty. At this point, the adrenal and pituitary glands secrete hormones (**androgen for boys** and **estrogen for girls**) that cause the visible secondary sex characteristics and the growth spurt.

JEAN PIAGET: COGNITIVE DEVELOPMENT

Piaget is such a major player in developmental psychology and so favored by the GRE Psychology Subject Test that you should expect several questions about him. Piaget is best known for his work with child developmental issues, in particular his theory of child cognitive development. He asserted that humans experience an interaction between internal maturation and external experience that creates qualitative change. This **adaptation** happens through **assimilation** (fitting new information into existing ideas) and **accommodation** (modification of cognitive schemata to incorporate new information). All children go through the following stages during cognitive development, and while the age may vary, the order of the stages does not:

Jean Piaget

STAGE	AGE	CHARACTERISTICS
Sensorimotor	0–2 yrs	First, Reflexive behavior cued by sensations; then **circular reactions** (repeated behavior intended to manipulate environment); later, development of **object permanence** (knowing an object exists even when it can no longer be seen); finally, acquiring the use of **representation (visualizing or putting words to objects)**
Preoperational	2–7 yrs	Egocentric understanding; rapidly acquiring words as symbols for things; inability to perform mental operations, such as causality or true understanding of quantity
Concrete Operational	7–12 yrs	Understanding of concrete relationships, such as simple math and quantity; development of **conservation** (knowing changes in shape are not changes in volume)
Formal Operational	12+ yrs	Understanding of abstract relationships, such as logic, ratios, and values

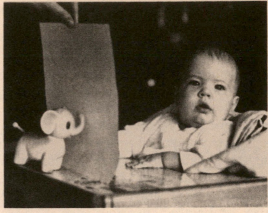

Courtesy George Zimbel/Monkmeyer

Lack of object permanence, or just an aversion to white paper?

Piaget suggested that the progress of language development was determined by the individual's current cognitive stage.

Rochel Gelman showed that Piaget might have underestimated the cognitive ability of preschoolers. Gelman said they can deal with ideas such as quantity in small sets of objects.

Piaget also dabbled with **moral development** in children. In *Moral Judgment of the Child*, he hypothesized three stages:

AGE	CHARACTERISTICS
4–7 yrs	Imitates rule-following behavior; does not question acceptance of rules
7–11 yrs	Understands rules and follows them
12+ yrs	Applies abstract thinking to rules; can change rules if all parties agree

SIGMUND FREUD: PERSONALITY DEVELOPMENT

Freud saw the driving force behind humans (and their development) as sexual. For Freud, this force meant sensual gratification and not just "sex." So his five stages of development deal with how the individual meets these sensual gratification or **biological needs**. Advancing through the stages affects personality development. Parental over- or underindulgence at a particular stage might result in **fixation** (inability to move on to the next stage). Later, life stressors might result in **regression** (a return to an earlier stage).

STAGE	AGE	CHARACTERISTICS
Oral	Birth–18 mos	Receives pleasure orally through sucking, eating, biting
Anal	18 mos–3 yrs	Receives pleasure with the control and release of feces
Phallic	3–6 yrs	Receives pleasure from self-stimulation of genitals. Boys develop an **Oedipus Complex** (jealous of father, in love with mother); girls develop an **Electra Complex** (angry with mother, in love with father because of **penis envy**); both resolve this conflict at the end of this stage by identifying with the same-sex parent. Boys are motivated to suppress their lust by **castration anxiety** (fear of castration)
Latency	adolescence	Repressed sexuality; identification with same-sex friends; focus on school and growing up
Genital	adolescence–adulthood	Hormones reawaken sexual instincts; love object is now nonfamilial

LAWRENCE KOHLBERG: MORAL DEVELOPMENT

Kohlberg created the best-known theory of moral development through analyzing responses of children to nine hypothetical moral dilemmas. One example is the **Heinz Dilemma**, in which a woman is dying and needs an expensive medication. Because the woman's husband cannot afford the medication, the dilemma is whether he should steal it or let his wife die. Using responses to such dilemmas, Kohlberg discerned the progress of moral understanding.

STAGE	UNDERSTANDING OF MORALS
Preconventional/Premoral "If I steal the medicine, I'll get in trouble."	Level 1: should avoid punishment Level 2: should gain rewards
Conventional/Morality of Conformity "Stealing is against the law."	Level 3: should gain approval Level 4: should follow law and authority
Postconventional/Morality of Self-Accepted Principles "It is unjust that money is an obstacle to life. It is ethical that I save my wife."	Level 5: beyond the black and white of laws; attentive to rights and social welfare Level 6: makes decisions based on abstract ethical principles

Carol Gilligan asserted that Kohlberg's moral development theory was biased toward males because it was dominated by rules, whereas women's morality focuses more on compassion.

ERIK ERIKSON: LIFE SPAN DEVELOPMENT

Erikson is best known for a development scheme that addresses the entire life span. Erikson viewed each stage of life as having its own unique **pyschosocial** conflict to resolve.

AGE	STAGE CRISIS	RESOLUTION
Birth–18 mos	**trust vs. mistrust**	trust
18 mos–3 yrs	**autonomy vs. shame and doubt**	independence
3–6 yrs	**initiative vs. guilt**	purpose
6–puberty	**industry vs. inferiority**	competency
Teen yrs	**identity vs. role confusion** (gave rise to the term **"identity crisis"**)	sense of self
Young adult	**intimacy vs. isolation**	love
Middle age	**productivity vs. stagnation**	productivity and caring
Old age	**ego integrity vs. despair**	wisdom and integrity

OTHER THINGS YOU SHOULD KNOW

- **John Bowlby** suggested that infants are motivated to attach to their mothers for **positive** reasons (wanting closeness) and for **negative** reasons (avoiding fear). Bowlby emphasized the importance of the mother-infant attachment during the infant's sensitive period to prevent character and stability problems.

- **Mary Ainsworth** studied attachment through the use of the **strange situation**. The strange situation consists of mother and infant (aged eight months to two years) playing together in a laboratory as researchers watch through a one-way mirror. Ainsworth studied different situations but found that overall, infants cried when a stranger entered the room (**stranger anxiety**) and when their mothers left the room (**separation anxiety**). Ainsworth also found that children responded differently to their mothers returning to the room. **Securely attached** infants ran and clung to their mothers. **Ambivalent** infants ignored or avoided their mothers. **Avoidant** infants squirmed or kicked if their mothers tried to comfort them. Also, it has been determined that securely attached infants more readily explore their environment than insecurely attached infants. Ainsworth's work has been carried on by Mary Main.

- **Diana Baumrind** studied the relationship between parenting style and personality development. **Authoritarian parents** (demanding, unaffectionate, strict) had children who were withdrawn and unhappy. **Permissive parents** (affectionate, not strict) had children who were happy but lacking in self-control and self-reliance. **Authoritative parents** (affectionate, firm but fair) had self-reliant, self-confident, assertive, friendly, happy, high-functioning kids. Authoritative parents help children understand and accept the norms of society so that they function well within it.

- **John Watson's behavioristic** approach to development asserted that children were passively molded by the environment and that their behavior emerges through **imitation** of their parents.

- Motor development through the first two years of life is largely controlled by **internal, maturational** factors. But countless studies have shown that **interacting with infants** through attention and affection fosters their physical, emotional, and intellectual development. Neglected children in institutions and orphanages show higher incidences of mental retardation and mortality, and poorer physical development.

- **Arnold Gessell** was an early child developmentalist who believed that nature provided only a "blueprint for development" through maturation and that environment or nurture filled in the details.

- Children identified as aggressive at an early age have a moderate tendency to remain aggressive through later life.

- **Sex-typed behavior** (behavior that seems stereotypical for gender) is low during prepubescence, highest in young adulthood, and lower again in later life.

- Boys who reach puberty sooner rather than later have been shown to be psychologically and socially advantaged.

- Adolescents most often have educational and career aspirations like those of their parents.

- A **hermaphrodite** or **intersex** individual is someone born with both female and male genitals. This is most likely the result of a female fetus being exposed to a higher than normal level of testosterone.

Study Tip: Make a separate list of the concepts that just won't stick in your memory. Rewriting the information will help.

15
Personality

DEFINED: **Personality is the study of why people act the way that they do and why different people act differently.** Personality theory is necessarily bound up in clinical theory, so a great deal of information about personality can be found in the Clinical Psychology chapter. For example, Freud's theory asserted that personality is what emerges from the struggle between the ego, id, and superego. (For more on Freud, turn to the Clinical and Developmental Psychology chapters.) In fact, all of the clinical theorists mentioned in the Clinical Psychology chapter necessarily have their own slant on personality. You should know these. But to avoid redundancy, those clinical theorists are not covered in this chapter.

OLD SCHOOL: TYPE THEORY

Type theory originally dominated personality theory. As far back as Hippocrates, people were placed into personality-type categories often based on physical appearance. In the 1800s, **phrenology** (the practice of examining head and skull shape) was used to discern personality.

Later, **William Sheldon** devised a system based on **somatotypes** (body types). Although the theory has no modern credence, it is an important part of the evolution of the field. Sheldon isolated three physiques and the corresponding personality types:

- **Endomorph**—short, plump body = pleasure-seeking, social behavior.

- **Mesomorph**—muscular, athletic body = energetic, aggressive behavior.

- **Ectomorph**—skinny, fragile body = inhibited, intellectual behavior.

More recently than Sheldon, **Alfred Adler** suggested a personality typology (see Clinical Psychology chapter). For the most part, however, type theories have given way to trait theories.

NEW SCHOOL: TRAIT THEORY

Gordon Allport emphasized an **ideographic** approach to personality theory. This approach attempts to capture an individual's unique, defining characteristics, opposed to a **nomothetic** approach, which uses large numbers of people to study the commonalities of personality. Allport was concerned only with conscious motives governed by the **proprium** or **propriate function** (his version of the ego), and he believed that the proprium acted somewhat consistently based on traits it had developed through experience.

Allport and his students worked to identify all of the possible traits that could go with personality. **Traits** are the relatively stable characteristics of behavior that a person exhibits, such as introversion, politeness, and stinginess. Using a **lexical approach** (meaning picking all of the possible traits out of the dictionary), Allport gathered about 5,000 possible traits. Next, Allport hypothesized that people act differently in different situations because they have a trait hierarchy: at the top a **cardinal** trait, then **central** traits, then **secondary** traits. So while circumstances may cause a person to show conflicting secondary traits, he will always be consistent with his cardinal trait. (In trait theory, be sure to understand the difference between **traits** and **states**. Traits are relatively enduring characteristics. States are temporary feelings or characteristics. A trait might be "outgoing," whereas a state might be "tired").

Later, statistical techniques were used to create **taxonomies** (organized categorization systems) for personality. Most importantly, **Raymond Cattell** used factor analysis in data reduction of Allport's 5,000 traits. Eventually, he identified **sixteen bipolar source traits**, such as relaxed-tense, that seemed to underlie all of the 5,000 (often overlapping) traits. These were Cattell's **sixteen personality factors** tested in his sixteen personality questionnaire. Amazingly, Cattell accomplished this massive factor analysis before the computer age.

Later, using advanced computer statistical programs, modern theorists could not replicate Cattell's findings, but they did generate findings of their own. The hot topic in personality trait theory today is the "**Big Five**." The Big Five are **superfactors**, or five dimensions that seem to encompass all of personality. They are superordinate traits or facets. Know these Big Five dimensions:

1. **O-dimension** (openness to experience, intellectual curiosity)

2. **C-dimension** (conscientiousness)

3. **E-dimension** (extroversion, enthusiasm)

4. **A-dimension** (agreeableness)

5. **N-dimension** (neuroticism, nervousness)

WHERE DOES PERSONALITY COME FROM?

Originally personality theory was dominated by **dispositionists** (people who emphasized internal determinants of behavior). Of course, **situationists** (such as behaviorists) have argued that only circumstances determine behavior. Currently, **interactionists** are in the forefront; they assert a combination of stable, internal factors and situations.

Evidence for both disposition and situation exits. Critics such as **Seymour Epstein** and **Walter Mischel** have asserted that trait and type theories have always had a big problem: Both theories assume that a person's behavior is stable across situations and that people fail to take circumstances into account. Studies (and real life) show that people often act differently in different situations. The possibility a person may behave inconsistently—that a respected minister may be a closet adulterer, for example—is called the **consistency paradox** and presents real problems for labeling people as having one internal disposition.

One way of showing that personality traits exist within a person would be to show that the person exhibits those traits in a variety of different situations. Mischel, with **Nancy Cantor**, proposed the **cognitive prototype approach**, in which cognitive behavior (such as the formulation of and attention to prototypes), is examined in social situations. In short, Mischel thought that consistency of behavior is the result of cognitive processes, rather than the result of personality traits per se.

Twin studies have indicated that the heritability of personality is about 40–50 percent. After locating identical twins separated at birth, psychologists have found remarkable similarities in personality and behavior. Most notably, the "Jim" twins had wives with the same name, dogs with the same name, and the same habits. But, of course, they were not exactly the same, and this shows that environment has some impact on personality.

GENDER DIFFERENCES

The **nature-nurture debate** is most alive in the area of gender differences. Some assert that no true gender differences exist—children are simply reinforced for stereotypical behaviors. It is true that after taking into account differential social reinforcement, very few gender differences remain. Still, the prevailing point of view is **interactionist**.

- **Kay Deaux** found that **women's successes** at stereotypical "male" tasks are often attributed to **luck**, while **men's successes** are often attributed to skill. This suggests that gender is a social construct that colors interpretations. Also, studies have found that women themselves attribute their successes to luck more than men, indicating that women have **lower self-esteem** than men.

- **Sandra Bem** studied **androgyny** (possessing both male and female qualities) and created the **Bem Sex Role Inventory**. Androgenous individuals have been found to have higher self-esteem, lower anxiety, and more adaptability than their highly masculine or feminine counterparts.

- **Matina Horner** suggested that females shunned masculine-type successes not because of fear of failure or lack of interest. Rather, women **feared success** and its negative repercussions, such as resentment and rejection.

- **Alice Eagly** found an interaction between gender and social status with regard to how easily an individual might be influenced or swayed.

- **Eleanor Maccoby** and **Carol Jacklin** scrutinized studies of sex differences and found that relatively few existed that could not be explained away by simple social learning. The most consistent difference that seems independent of social influence is that **females have greater verbal ability** and **males have greater visual/spatial ability**. This has been attributed to internal biological or hormonal differences but is still hotly debated.

- Women are twice as likely as men to become depressed.

OTHER THINGS YOU SHOULD KNOW

- **Meyer Friedman** and **Ray Rosenman** studied Type A personality. **Type A personality** is characterized by drive, competitiveness, aggressiveness, and tension and is most commonly found in middle-to-upper-class men. **Grant Dahlstrom** linked Type A personality to heart disease and other health problems. The connection between personality and health is currently a popular vein of study.

- **Hans Eysenck** used factor analysis to identify the traits underneath the two personality-type dimensions of **introversion-extraversion** and **stable-unstable (neuroticism)**. These two dimensions formed a cross and, therefore, four quadrants: **phlegmatic, melancholic, choleric,** and **sanguine**.

- **Learned helplessness**, the brainchild of **Martin Seligman**, demonstrates how experience can change people's personalities. After a series of events in which one may feel helpless or out of control, a negative or pessimistic explanatory style develops. The person basically gives up in general and exhibits a helpless disposition. This can be countered with cognitive training that fosters **learned optimism** for the person.

- **Multiplicative observation** is the method of discerning personality from a variety of observations and situations.

- **Authoritarianism** is the disposition to view the world as full of power relationships. Authoritarian individuals are highly domineering (if they are the top dog of the situation) or highly submissive (if they are in the presence of a more powerful figure). These individuals are also likely conventional, aggressive, stereotyping, and anti-introspective. This is measured by the **F-scale** (also known as the Fascism Scale).

- **Stimulus-seeking** individuals have a great need for arousal.

- People often make assumptions about the dispositions of an individual based on the actions of that person. These are known as **implicit theories** about personality.

- **George Kelley** suggested that **personal constructs** (conscious ideas about the self, others, and situations) determine personality and behavior.

- **Self-handicapping** is self-defeating behavior that allows one to dismiss or excuse failure.

- **Seymour Epstein** was critical of personality trait theory.

- A **phenomenological view** of personality theory (or of psychotherapy) focuses on the individual's unique **self** and experiences.

- **Self-monitoring** is characterized by scrutiny of one's own behavior, motivation to act appropriately rather than honestly, and ability to mask true feelings.

- **Barnum effect** is the tendency to agree with and accept **personality interpretations** that are provided.

- **External locus of control** is a personality characteristic that causes one to view events as the result of luck or fate. Too much of this breeds helplessness. **Internal locus of control** causes a person to view events as the outcome of her own actions. Too much of this can breed self-blame. These terms were developed by **Julian Rotter**.

- **Dispositional attribution** is the tendency for others to think that actions are caused more by a person's personality than by the situation. This would mean that a person lies because she is a liar, not because of the pull of the situation. This is also known as the **fundamental attribution error**.

- **Self-awareness** is a **state**; it is the temporary condition of being aware of how you are thinking, feeling, or doing. For example, right now you may be aware that you are nervous.

- **Self-consciousness** is a **trait**. It refers to how often one generally becomes self-aware. If you pay a lot of attention to yourself, then you are highly self-conscious.

- **Mirrors** generally make people more self-aware. **Small mirrors** tend not to make people highly self-aware because we see ourselves in small mirrors all the time (e.g. in the bathroom). But large mirrors make people very self-aware because we see a view of ourselves as others see us.

- **Narcissism** is not the same as self-esteem. Narcissism is believing that you are better than you really are or look better than you really do; it is a sort of unrealistic self-esteem. A narcissistic person might endorse the statement, "The world would be a better place if I were in charge."

- **Self-esteem** is knowing that you are worthwhile and being in touch with your actual strengths. About 50 percent of people perceive themselves accurately and about 35 percent perceive themselves narcissistically.

- Personality tests come in all shapes and sizes. Probably the two best known are the **Minnesota Multiphasic Personality Inventory (MMPI)** and the **California Personality Inventory (CPI)**. For more on these tests, see the Measurement chapter.

- **Henry Murray** developed the **Thematic Apperception Test (TAT)**. This test consists of ambiguous story cards. Murray asserted that people would project their own "needs" onto these cards, such as the need for achievement.

- **Costa and McCrae** found that personality changes very little after age **30**.

- **Abraham Malsow** created the **hierarchy of needs**. For more on this, see the Clinical Psychology chapter.

Study Tip: The acronym OCEAN will help you remember the Big Five!

16

Social Psychology

DEFINED: Social psychology is the study of how people relate to and influence each other. Social psychology uses the experimental method to study individuals (whereas sociology is more interested in studying groups). Social Psychology is one of the most heavily weighted sections on the test, so learn your research studies! Some have alleged that social psychology is simply common sense about what we see every day. Let that help you. Use your common sense when choosing answers about social psychology findings.

BIG WIGS

This field overflows with big wig researchers and their studies. They have been subdivided into research areas below—know them all. Three founding big wigs:

- **Norman Triplett** conducted the first official social psychology type experiment in 1897 on social facilitation. He found that cyclists performed better when paced by others than when they rode alone.

- **Kurt Lewin** is considered by many to be the founder of the field of social psychology. He applied Gestalt ideas to social behavior. He conceived **field theory,** which is the total of influences upon individual behavior. A person's **life space** is the collection of forces upon the individual. **Valence**, **vector**, and **barrier** are forces in the life space (see Learning).

- **Fritz Heider** was the founder of:

  - **Attribution Theory**, or the study of how people infer the causes of others' behavior. People will actually attribute intentions and emotions to just about anything—even moving geometrical shapes on a screen!

  - **Balance Theory,** or the study of how people make their feelings and/ or actions consistent to preserve psychological homeostasis.

MISTAKES WE MAKE

- **Fundamental attribution error** is the common tendency to think that the actions of others result from internal disposition rather than situation. ("Jane lied because she is a liar!") Predictably, we go easier on ourselves and attribute our own behavior to circumstance.

- **Actor-observer attributional divergence** is the tendency for the person who is doing the behavior to have a different perspective on the situation than a person watching the behavior.

- **Self-serving bias** is interpreting one's own actions and motives in a positive way, blaming situations for failures and taking credit for successes. We like to think we are "better than average."

- **Illusory correlation** is assuming that two unrelated things have a relationship.

- **Hindsight bias** is believing after the fact that you knew something all along.

- **Halo effect** is thinking that if someone has one good quality then he has only good qualities.

- **Self-fulfilling prophecy** occurs when one's expectations somehow draw out, or in a sense cause, the very behavior that is expected.

- **False consensus bias** is assuming most other people think as you do.

- **Lee Ross** studied subjects who were first made to believe a statement and then later told it was false. The subjects continued to believe the statement if they had processed it and devised their own logical explanation for it.

- **Richard Nisbett** showed that we lack awareness for why we do what we do.

- **Base-rate fallacy** is overestimating the general frequency of things we are most familiar with.

- **M. J. Lerner's just world bias** is the belief that good things happen to good people and bad things happen to bad people. It is uncomfortable for people to accept that bad things happen to good people, so they blame the victim.

- **Ellen Langer** studied the **illusion of control**, or belief that you can control things that you actually have no influence on. This illusion is the driving force behind manipulating the lottery, gambling, and superstition.

- **Oversimplification** is the tendency to make simple explanations for complex events. People also hold onto original ideas about cause even when new factors emerge.

- **Representativeness heuristic** is using a shortcut about typical assumptions to guess at an answer rather than relying on actual logic. For example, one might assume that a woman who is six feet tall and beautiful is more likely to be a model rather than a lawyer, even though there are many more lawyers than models.

WHY WE DO WHAT WE DO

- **Leon Festinger's cognitive dissonance theory** suggests that it is uncomfortable for people to have beliefs that do not match their actions. After making a difficult decision, people are motivated to back their actions up by touting corresponding beliefs. Also, the less the act is justified by circumstance, the more we feel the need to justify it by bringing our attitude in line with the behavior.

- **Daryl Bem's self-perception theory** offers an alternative explanation to cognitive dissonance. Bem asserted that when people are unsure of their beliefs, they take their cues from their own behavior (rather than actually changing their beliefs to match their actions). For example, if a man demanded $1,000 to work on a Saturday, he would probably realize that he does not like his job all that much.

- **Overjustification effect** follows from self-perception theory. It is the tendency to assume that we must not want to do things that we are paid or compensated to do. A person who loves to sing and is then paid to do so will lose pleasure in singing because the activity is now overjustified.

- **Gain-loss theory** suggests that people act in order to obtain gain and avoid loss. People feel most favorably toward situations that start out negatively but end positively (even when compared to completely positive situations).

- **Social exchange theory** suggests that humans interact in ways that maximize reward and minimize costs.

- **Self-presentation**, particularly positive self-presentation, is an important influence on behavior. We act in ways that are in line with our attitudes or in ways that will be accepted by others.

    - **Self-monitoring** is the process by which people pay close attention to their actions. Often, as a result, people change their behaviors to be more favorable.

    - **Impression management** is behaving in ways that might make a good impression.

- **Social facilitation** is the tendency for the presence of others to either enhance or hinder performance. **Robert Zajonc** found that the presence of others helps with easy tasks but hinders complex tasks.

- **Social comparison** is evaluating one's own actions, abilities, opinions, and ideas by comparing them to those of others. Because these "others" are generally familiar people from our own social group or strata, social comparison has been used as an argument against **mainstreaming**. When children with difficulties are thrown into classes with children without such difficulties, this comparison may result in lower self-esteem for the children with problems.

- **Role** is the set of behavior norms that seem suitable for a particular person.

- **Morton Deutsch** used the **prisoner's dilemma** and the **trucking company game** story to illustrate the struggle between cooperation and competition. The premise of the prisoner's dilemma is that, if two criminal cohorts are detained separately and charged with the crime, the best strategy is for neither to talk. This way, no information will be given. But because a person can never be sure what the other might do (perhaps plea bargain and testify against him), remaining silent is a gamble that requires trust. Therefore, most people spill the beans when they should simply remain silent. The Trucking Company Game describes two companies that can choose to cooperate (and agree on high fixed prices) or compete against each other with lower prices. The best strategy would be to cooperate and agree on high prices, but because one company cannot totally trust the other, they choose to compete. It's the same as the prisoner's dilemma but in economic terms.

- **Equity Theory** is the idea that people feel most comfortable in situations in which rewards and punishments are equal, fitting, or highly logical. **Overbenefited** people tend to feel guilty. Random or illogical punishments make people anxious.

- **Stanley Milgram's Stimulus-Overload Theory** explains why urbanites are less prosocial than country people are; urbanites don't need any more interaction.

- **Reciprocal interaction**, or the constant exchange of influences between people, is a constant factor in our behavior.

POWER PLAYS

- **Conformity** is going along with real or perceived group pressure. People may go along publicly but not privately (**compliance**), or change actions and beliefs to conform (**acceptance**). An individual who speaks out against the majority is a **dissenter**. An individual is most likely to conform when:

  - There is a majority opinion.

  - The majority has a unanimous position.

  - The majority has high status, or the individual is concerned with her own status.

  - The situation is in public.

  - The individual was not previously committed to another position.

  - The individual has low self-esteem.

  - The individual scores high on a measure of authoritarianism.

- **Reactance** is the refusal to conform that may occur as a result of a blatant attempt to control. Also, people will often not conform if they are **forewarned** that others will attempt to change them.

- **Stanley Milgram** is known for his very famous study in which subjects were ordered to administer "painful electrical shock" to others in an adjacent room. These others were confederates (fakers who were in on the experiment). The experiment explored how people responded to the orders of others. Conditions that facilitated conformity were remoteness of the victim, a legitimate-seeming commander, and the conformity of other subjects. Males went along about 66 percent of the time. This type of experiment has been used to explain the actions of Nazi war criminals.

- **Philip Zimbardo** later found that people who were wearing hoods (and so deindividuated) were more willing to administer higher levels of shock than people without hoods. Also, in his classic prison simulation experiments, Zimbardo found that normal subjects could easily be transformed into sadistic prison guards. In both cases, Zimbardo showed that people will step into some surprising roles.

- **Solomon Asch** had subjects listen to the staged "opinion" of others about which lines on a board were equal. The subjects then gave their own opinion. Subjects conformed to the clearly incorrect opinion of others about 33 percent of the time. The unanimity seemed to be the influential factor.

- **Muzafer Sherif**'s classic experiment found that people's descriptions of the autokinetic effect (see Perception) were influenced by others' descriptions.

- An individual speaker is most likely to change a listener's attitude if:

  - The speaker is an expert and/or trustworthy.

  - The speaker is similar to the listener.

  - The speaker is acceptable to the listener.

  - The speaker is overheard rather than obviously trying to influence.

  - The content is anecdotal, emotional, or shocking.

  - The speaker is part of a two-person debate rather than a one-sided argument.

- **R. E. Petty** and **J. T. Cacioppo's elaboration likelihood** model of persuasion suggests that people who are very involved in an issue listen to the strength of the arguments in the issue rather than more superficial factors, such as the characteristics of the speaker.

- **Sleeper effect** explains why persuasive communication from a source of low credibility may become more acceptable after the fact.

- **McGuire's inoculation theory** asserts that people's beliefs are vulnerable if they have never faced challenge. Once they have experienced a challenge to their opinions, however, they are less vulnerable. Challenge is like a vaccination.

GROUPS

- **Deindividuation** occurs when individual identity or accountability is de-emphasized. This may be the result of mingling in a crowd, wearing uniforms, or otherwise adopting a larger group identity.

- **The Kitty Genovese case** (the murder of a woman witnessed by scores of people) led to the investigation of the **bystander effect**, or why people are less likely to help when others are present.

- **Diffusion of responsibility** is the tendency that the larger the group, the less likely individuals in the group will act or take responsibility. As in the Genovese case, the more bystanders nearby, the less likely anyone will help. Everyone waits for someone else to act. This is the result of deindividuation.

- **Social loafing** is the tendency to work less hard in a group as the result of diffusion of responsibility. It is guarded against when each individual is closely monitored.

- **Phil Zimbardo** found that antisocial behavior positively correlates with population density. He left a broken-down car in New York City and Palo Alto, California. A hidden camera recorded as the car in New York City was stripped and destroyed within 10 minutes. In Palo Alto, the car was untouched for three days.

- **Competition** for scarce resources usually causes conflict in a group. **Muzafer Sherif** showed that win/lose game-type competition can also trigger serious conflict in groups. **Sherif's Robbers' cave experiment** (a study about prejudice) showed that group conflict is most effectively overcome by the need for cooperative attention to a higher **superordinate** goal.

- **Contact** with the opposing party decreases conflict. We fear what we do not know.

- **Group polarization**, studied by **James Stoner**, is the concept that group discussion generally serves to strengthen the already dominant point of view. This explains the **risky shift**, or why groups will take greater risks than individuals.

- **Groupthink**, studied by **Irving Janis**, is likely to occur in a group that has unquestioned beliefs, pressure to conform, invulnerability, censors, cohesiveness within, isolation from without, and a strong leader.

- **Kenneth** and **Mamie Clark** conducted the famous **doll preference studies**, which factored into the 1954 Supreme Court case, *Brown v. the Board of Education*. The studies demonstrated the negative effects that group segregation had on African American children's self-esteem. The African American children thought the white dolls were better.

- **Ingroup/outgroup bias** is when individuals in one group think their members have more positive qualities and fewer negative qualities than the other group even though the qualities are the same in each. This is the basis for **prejudice**.

I SAY TOMATO

- In relative order of importance, we are attracted to other people who:
  1. Are near us, because then we get a chance to know them (propinquity)
  2. Are physically attractive
  3. Have similar attitudes
  4. Like us back (reciprocity)
- **Opposites do not attract**. The old saying is just talk, according to research.
- **Reciprocity of disclosure**, or sharing secrets/feelings, facilitates emotional closeness.
- **Mere-exposure effect** is how stimuli are rated. The more we see or experience something, the more positively we rate it.

OTHER THINGS YOU SHOULD KNOW

- **Richard Lazarus** studied stress and coping. He differentiated between problem-focused coping (which is changing the stressor) and emotion-focused coping (which is changing our response to a stressor).
- **Objective self-awareness** is achieved through self-perception, high self-monitoring, internality, and self-efficacy. Some experimenters will facilitate objective self-awareness by having subjects perform tasks while looking in a mirror. Deindividuation would work against objective self-awareness.
- **Door-in-the-face** is a sales tactic in which people ask for more than they would ever get and then "settle" for less (the realistic amount hoped for).
- **Foot-in-the-door phenomenon** is how doing a small favor makes people more willing to do larger ones later.
- **Social support network** effects on mental health have emerged as an area of study that combines social and clinical ideas.
- **J. Rodin** and **E. Langer** showed that nursing home residents who have plants to care for have better health and lower mortality rates.
- **Bogus pipeline** is an instrument that measures physiological reactions in order to measure the truthfulness of attitude self-reporting.
- **Peter Principle** is the concept that people are promoted at work until they reach a position of incompetence, the position in which they remain.

- **Stuart Valins** studied environmental influences on behavior. Architecture matters. Students in long-corridor dorms feel more stressed and withdrawn than students in suite-style dorms.

- **Leonard Berkowitz's Frustration-Aggression Hypothesis** posits a relationship between frustration in achieving a goal (no matter how small) and the show of aggression.

- **M. Rokeach** studied racial bias and the similarity of beliefs. People prefer to be with like-minded people more than with like-skinned people. Also, racial bias decreases as attitude similarity between people increases.

- **M. Fischbein** and **I. Ajzen** are known for their work on attitudes. They found that general attitudes will not predict specific behavior, but specific, relevant attitudes will predict specific behavior.

- **Cross-cultural research** is more popular now than ever. Much of it revolves around determining whether Western ways of conceptualizing or behaving are the same as the ways of other cultures. For example, **Hazel Markus** has found that Eastern countries, in contrast to Western, value interdependence over independence. In countries in which interdependence is emphasized (such as Japan), individuals are more likely to demonstrate conformity, modesty, and pessimism. In countries where independence is emphasized (such as the US), individuals are more likely to show optimism, self-enhancement, and individuality. Some have criticized this research for making generalizations about cultures.

- An **attitude** is a positive, negative, or neutral evaluation of a person, issue, or object.

- **Elaine Hatfield** and other researchers have looked at different kinds of love. According to Hatfield, the two basic types of love are passionate love and companionate love. **Passionate love** is intense longing for the union with another and a state of profound physiological arousal. **Companionate love** is the affection we feel for those with whom our lives are deeply entwined. Passionate love, which is based on a biophysiological system shared with other primates, is a powerful emotion that can be both positive (when love is reciprocal) and negative (when love is unrequited). Companionate love, on the other hand, is achieved via mutual trust, respect, and commitment and often characterizes later stages of relationships.

- **Paul Ekman** has argued that humans have six basic emotions: **sadness**, **happiness**, **fear**, **anger**, **surprise**, and **disgust**. He drew this conclusion from cross-cultural studies that show that individuals in a variety of different cultures were able to recognize facial expressions corresponding to the six aforementioned emotions. Researchers code facial expressions for emotion using the Facial Action Coding System or **FACS coding**. Such coding can help determine whether a smile is genuine (derived from happiness and therefore engaging the upper cheek) or whether it is fake (a smile is made with the mouth but the eyes and whole face are less involved).

- **Reciprocal socialization** is when two parties (such as parents and children) adapt to or are socialized by each other. For example, we say that parents or adults are socialized by youngsters when parents pick up new lingo, such as "phat," and that children are socialized by parents when children learn to respect rules and traditions.

> **Study Tip:** Not surprisingly, people change their attitude about activities or interests once these interests become a paying job. According to the overjustification effect, getting paid for something you enjoy often leads to reduced enjoyment. Before you apply to graduate school, do some work in the field. This will both help your application and let you see how your interests hold up as a job.

17

History of Psychology

DEFINED: The history of psychology extends from philosophy to current thought. Though psychology is a relatively new science, its roots extend deeply into philosophy. For centuries, debates regarding the nature of existence and the mind entangled philosophers. These cumbersome issues were examined from philosophical and, later, physiological angles until finally a new field emerged to focus exclusively on these questions.

ANCIENT GREEKS (B.C.)

- **Socrates** was the original philosophic mentor who pondered the abstract ideas of truth, beauty, and justice.

- **Plato** was Socrates' pupil. Plato declared that the physical world was not all that could be known. He asserted the presence of universal forms and innate knowledge. Plato's philosophy was abstract and unsystematic.

- **Aristotle**, Plato's pupil, is recognized as the world's first professor. His studies were based on order and logic. Unlike Plato, Aristotle believed that truth would be found in the physical world.

MIDDLE AGES (500–1600)

During the Middle Ages, philosophy changed hands twice. Understanding the mysterious world temporarily became a question for the church. Then, at the brink of the modern world, philosophy was reclaimed by scholars.

SCIENTIFIC REVOLUTION (1600–1700)

The scientific revolution created the world we know today. Major discoveries shaped the way people viewed existence. First, we figured out that the earth was not the center of the universe (oops!), and this made man a mere part of the big machine rather than the operator (ouch!). Nothing was the same again. Meanwhile, philosophy was back in the hands of scholars, and they all had different ideas about the nature of things.

- **René Descartes** said **"I think, therefore I am."** His focus was figuring out truths through reason and deduction. He pondered dualism or the **mind-body problem**.

- **John Locke** is famous for asserting that, upon entering the world, man's mind is a **tabula rasa** or blank slate. He asserted that what we know and what we are comes from experience. Knowledge was not innate.

- **Thomas Hobbes** asserted that humans and other animals were machines and that sense-perception was all that could be known. From this, he suggested that a science could be formed to explain people just as physics explained the machines of the world.

ENLIGHTENMENT (1700–1800)

After the scientific revolution, many were sold on science and reason although some held fast to metaphysics. In the 18th century, understanding the mind supplanted understanding existence as the most important question of the time. A familiar debate continued: **Immanuel Kant** countered Locke's previous claim by asserting that our minds were active, not passive.

THE BRINK OF PSYCHOLOGY (1800–1900)

By the 1800s, psychology (the study of the mind) was the pressing issue for philosophers and physiologists alike. So many professionals were preoccupied with unlocking the secrets of the mind that by the end of the century, psychology emerged as a distinct field.

- **Anton Mesmer (1734–1815)** was the Viennese creator of a kind of popular science. He believed that the healing of physical ailments came from the manipulation of people's bodily fluids. He thought that "animal magnetism" (the mind control of one person over another) was responsible for his patients' recoveries. Mesmer's technique of **mesmerism** began to be used by others under the general term of hypnotism (hence, the term "mesmerized," which means hypnotized).

- **Franz Joseph Gall (1758–1828)** used ideas from physiology and philosophy to create a "science" later termed **phrenology**. Phrenology was the idea that the nature of a person could be known by examining the shape and contours of the skull. Because Gall saw the brain as the seat of the soul, certain features on the head were said to be indicators of particular personality traits. **J. Spurzheim** carried on Gall's work even though other scientists proved the theory incorrect.

- **Charles Darwin (1809–1882)** wrote *Origin of Species* (1859) and *The Descent of Man* (1871). Though he did not create the concept of evolution, he made evolution a scientifically sound principle by positing that natural selection was its driving force (see Ethology).

- **Sir Francis Galton (1822–1911)** was an independently wealthy Englishman who traveled extensively and studied various things for fun. As a result, he made important, but random, contributions to psychology. Galton was the first to use statistics in psychology, and he created the correlation coefficient. Most notably, he wrote *Hereditary Genius* (1869) and used Darwinian principles to promote **eugenics**. Eugenics was a plan for selective human breeding in order to strengthen the species.

- **Gustav Fechner (1801–1887)** is credited with the founding of experimental psychology because of his work *Elements of Psychophysics* (1860). Fechner had carried out the first systematic psychology experiment to result in mathematical conclusions. Previously, it was thought that the mind could not be studied empirically.

- **Johannes Müller (1801–1858)** was a German physiologist at the University of Berlin. He wrote *Elements of Physiology* (1842) and postulated the existence of "specific nerve energies." Wilhelm Wundt was a student of Müller.

- **Wilhelm Wundt (1832–1920)** is best known as the **founder of psychology**. He is credited with this title because he founded the first official laboratory for psychology at the University of Leipzig in 1879 and because he began the first psychology journal in 1881. He wrote *Principles of Physiological Psychology* (1873), and created a complicated psychology that attempted to study and analyze consciousness. His ideas were the forerunners of **Edward Titchener's**, but they received even less attention.

Courtesy Historical Pictures Service

Wilhelm Wundt (1832–1920)

- **Herbert Spencer (1820–1903)** wrote *Principles of Psychology* (1855) and became the father of the psychology of adaptation. (He is also the founder of sociology.) Spencer used principles from Lamarckian evolution, physiology, and associationism to understand people. He asserted that different species or races were elevated because of the greater number of associations that their brains could make.

- **William James (1842–1910)** is often called the father of experimental psychology. He was busy doing in America what Wundt was doing in Germany: combining the fields of physiology and philosophy into a new field. Though he was informally investigating psychological principles at Harvard University in the late 1870s, he did not officially have a lab or course dedicated to psychology until the 1880s (so Wundt just beat James to the punch as the founder of psychology). James' *Principles of Psychology* (1890) inspired American psychology in a way that writings from other countries had not. James wrote about the mind's **stream of consciousness** and about **functionalist** ideas that sharply contrasted with structuralist ideas of discrete conscious elements.

- **Hermann von Helmholtz (1821–1894)** was a natural scientist who studied sensation. Much of his work with hearing and color vision is the foundation for modern perception research. Like Wundt, he studied with Müller. (See Sensation.)

- **Stanley Hall (1842–1924)** was a student of James and received America's first Ph.D. in psychology from Harvard. He coined the term "adolescence," started the *American Journal of Psychology* (1887), and founded the **American Psychological Association** (1892).

- **John Dewey (1859–1952)** is recognized as one of America's most influential philosophers. He attempted to synthesize philosophy and psychology and is best known in psychology for his work on the **reflex arc**. Dewey denied that animals respond to their environment through disjointed stimulus and response chains. He asserted instead that animals are constantly adapting to their environment rather than processing isolated stimuli. This work was the foundation for **functionalism**. Drawn from Darwinian ideas, functionalism examined the adaptive nature of the mind and body through observational methods.

- **Edward Titchener (1867–1927)** taught at Cornell University and was the founder of **structuralism**. Structuralism focused on the analysis of human consciousness. Through **introspection**, lab assistants attempted to objectively describe the **discrete sensations** and contents of their minds. Titchener was an Englishman who studied with Wundt. The structuralist method dissolved after Titchener's death.

- **James Cattell (1860–1944)** was an American who studied with Hall, Galton, and Wundt. He opened psychology laboratories at the University of Pennsylvania and at Columbia University. He thought that psychology should be more scientific than Wundt did.

- **Dorthea Lynde Dix** spearheaded the 19th century movement to provide better care for the mentally ill through hospitalization.

THE SAGA CONTINUES (1900s)

With psychology now a science in its own right, the saga continues amongst new theorists. Are we more than what we learn? How can we explain the contents of our minds? What most effectively alters our thoughts and behaviors? Below you will find the most famous figures of the 1900s and the work for which they are best known. With a few exceptions, most of these figures are discussed at length in earlier chapters that cover their area of accomplishment.

- **Ivan Pavlov (1849–1936)** acquired fame as the winner of a Nobel Prize for work on digestion. In his later work investigating dogs and digestion, he accidentally uncovered the behavioral concept now called **classical conditioning**. (See Learning.)

- **John B. Watson (1878–1958)** was an American psychologist who expanded on the ideas of Pavlov and founded the school of **behavioralism**. Watson studied conditioning, stimulus-response chains, and objective, observable behaviors. He saw humans as "squirming bits of flesh" ready to be trained by the environment. (See Learning.) Hence, his quote:

> Give me a dozen healthy infants, well-formed, and my own
> specified world to bring them up in and I'll guarantee to take
> any one at random and train him to become any type of special-
> ist I might select. . .regardless of his talents, penchants, tenden-
> cies, abilities, vocations, and race of his ancestors.

- **Nature v. Nurture** (aka **evolutionary psychology v. social constructionism**) is the debate about whether psychological phenomena are the result of inborn, genetic factors or the result of cultural and societal influences. This is the oldest debate in psychology.

- **Edward Thorndike (1874–1949)** was a psychologist at Columbia University. His idea, the **Law of Effect**, was the precursor of operant conditioning. (See Learning and Comparative Psychology.)

- **B.F. Skinner (1904–1990)** was a famous behaviorist who studied the ideas of Thorndike and Watson. He is most known for his studies that used the **Skinner box** and that led to the principles of operant **conditioning**. His famous books *Walden Two* (1948) and *Beyond Freedom and Dignity* (1972) philosophically discussed the control of human behavior. (See Learning.)

- **Max Wertheimer**, **Wolfgang Kohler**, and **Kurt Koffka** forged the school of **Gestalt psychology** around the early 1900s in reaction to attempts to study the mind and experience in distinct parts. Gestalt psychology, coined from the German word that means "whole" or "form," asserts that in perception the whole is greater than the sum of its parts. (See Perception and Clinical Psychology.)

- **Sigmund Freud (1856–1939)** is one of the most important figures in clinical, abnormal, and personality psychology. He is most famous for his personality theory that advanced a three-part structure of the mind, known as the **id, ego,** and **superego**. What is most notable about his personality theory is the importance placed on **unconscious motivations**. Freud also began the form of psychotherapy called **psychoanalysis**. Finally, Freud made significant contributions to the fields of psychology and philosophy through various papers. His most famous writings are *The Interpretation of Dreams* (1900), *Three Essays on the Theory of Sexuality* (1905), *Beyond the Pleasure Principle* (1920), and *Civilization and its Discontents* (1930). (See Personality and Clinical Psychology.)

- **Alfred Adler (1870–1936)**, a colleague of Freud, eventually broke from Freud to create his own **individual psychology**. Adler asserted that people were largely motivated by **inferiority**. He also created a four-type theory of personality: **choleric** (dominant), **phlegmatic** (dependent), **melancholic** (withdrawn), and **sanguine** (healthy). (See Clinical Psychology and Personality.)

- **Carl Gustav Jung (1875–1961)**, Freud's most beloved student, broke from Freud because he felt that too much emphasis was placed on the **libido**, or sexual instinct. Jung's own movement evolved from his work with Freud and is called **analytic psychology**. Analytic psychology is best known for its metaphysical and mythological components, such as the **collective unconscious** and the unconscious **archetypes**. Jung's autobiography, *Memories, Dreams, Reflections* (1961) is standard required reading in undergraduate psychology. (See Clinical Psychology.)

- **Jean Piaget (1896–1980)**, a Swiss psychologist, is a significant figure in developmental psychology. His most important work concerned cognitive development in children. Piaget's three classic works are *The Language and Thought of the Child* (1926), *The Moral Judgment of the Child* (1933), and *The Origins of Intelligence in Children* (1952). (See Developmental Psychology.)

- **Clark Hull (1884–1952)** secured a place for himself in the history of psychology with his mechanistic behavioral ideas. Hull explained motivation using math: **Performance = Drive × Habit**. In other words, we do what we need to do and we do what has worked best in the past. **Kenneth Spence** later modified Hull's theory. (See Learning.)

- **Edward Tolman (1886–1959)** was a behaviorist who uniquely valued both behavior and cognition. Tolman asserted that rats in mazes formed **cognitive maps** rather than blindly attempting various routes. Tolman also created an **expectancy-value theory** of motivation in which **Performance = Expectation × Value**. (See Learning.)

- **Clinical psychology** emerged after World War II and changed psychology from a largely scientific field to a practical field as well. People wanted treatment, in addition to information, from psychology. Decades of research were transferred to practical techniques.

- **Konrad Lorenz (1903–1992),** is best known as the founder of ethology, was famous for his work with imprinting in ducklings. He also wrote *On Aggression* (1966). (See Ethology.)

- **Carl Rogers (1902–1987)** is famous for his creation of **client-centered therapy**. In Rogerian therapy, the **client** (not patient) directs the course of therapy and receives **unconditional positive regard** from the therapist. This therapy is classified as **humanistic** because of its positive view of humans. Rogers also made a contribution to research: He was the first to record his sessions for later study and reference. (See Clinical Psychology.)

- **Abraham Maslow (1908–1970)** was the leader of **humanistic** psychology. He examined normal or optimal functioning as opposed to abnormal functioning. He is best known for his development of the **hierarchy of needs**. Maslow argued that people inherently strive for self-improvement. (See Clinical Psychology.)

- **Erik Erikson (1902–1994)** postulated eight stages of psychosocial development. His theory has been noted for its completeness, because his stages span development from infancy through old age. Erikson coined the term **identity crisis** in naming the key crisis of adolescence. (See Developmental Psychology.)

- **Victor Frankl (1905–1997),** a key figure in **existential psychology**, wrote *Man's Search for Meaning* (1963). Existential psychology posits that people innately seek meaningfulness in their lives and that perceived meaninglessness is the root of emotional difficulty. Frankl devised **logotherapy**, a form of therapy that focuses on the person's **will to meaning**. (See Clinical Psychology.)

- **Aaron Beck (1921–)** is the figure most associated with **cognitive** therapeutic techniques. According to Beck and other cognitive theorists, problems arise from maladaptive ways of thinking about the world. Thus, cognitive therapy involves reformulating illogical cognitions rather than searching for a life-stress cause for these cognitions. Beck also wrote the **Beck Depression Inventory (BDI)**, which is widely used to assess the severity of depressive symptoms once a person has already been diagnosed as depressed. (See Clinical Psychology.)

Study Tip: Don't worry about the exact years in which notable figures in psychology lived. Use this information to make a time line. This way you can group important people temporally and better understand the history of psychology.

18

Applied
Psychology

DEFINED: Applied psychology is the branch of psychology that uses principles or research findings to solve people's problems. On recent tests, applied psychology has been limited to questions about the DSM-IV and APA publications. Remember that applied psychology will be tested with only one to three questions.

DIAGNOSTIC AND STATISTICAL MANUAL OF MENTAL DISORDERS, FOURTH EDITION (DSM-IV)

Diagnostic and Statistical Manual of Mental Disorders, fourth edition (DSM-IV) is brought to you by the American Psychiatric Association. It serves as psychology's diagnostic bible. Included in the DSM-IV are 16 separate categories of mental disorders, the diagnostic criteria for the various disorders included in each category, and the official numerical codes assigned to each disorder.

First published in 1952, the manual is intended for clinical, research, and educational use. The fourth and most current edition of the DSM was published in 1994. As you might expect, the amount of detail in the DSM-IV is quite overwhelming. Simply understand the overall structure of the manual and, if you have time, take a look at a DSM-IV at the library.

SIXTEEN CATEGORIES OF MENTAL DISORDERS (AND EXAMPLES OF EACH)

See the Abnormal Psychology chapter for more information.

1. Disorders usually first diagnosed in infancy, childhood, or adolescence (retardation, learning disability, developmental disorder, attention or tic disorders)

2. Delirium, dementia, and amnestic and other cognitive disorders (delirium and dementia related to Alzheimer's, Parkinson's, and alcoholism)

3. Mental disorders due to a general medical condition not elsewhere classified (mental symptoms that result from a genuine medical problem)

4. Substance-related disorders (dependence and abuse of alcohol, cannabis, cocaine, hallucinogens, nicotine, etc.)

5. Schizophrenia and other psychotic disorders (types of schizophrenia, psychotic disorders, hallucinations and delusions)

6. Mood disorders (depressive and bipolar disorders)

7. Anxiety disorders (panic, agoraphobia, other phobias, obsessive-compulsive, post-traumatic stress, anxiety)

8. Somatoform disorders (conversion disorder, hypochondriasis, formerly called "psychosomatic" disorders)

9. Factitious disorders (feigned or produced illness for attention)

10. Dissociative disorders (amnesia, fugue, identity disorder, depersonalization)

11. Sexual and gender identity disorders (desire, arousal, orgasmic, and sexual pain disorders)

12. Eating disorders (anorexia and bulimia)

13. Sleep disorders (dyssomnias, insomnia, hypersomnia, narcolepsy, sleep-walking, night terror)

14. Impulse-control disorders not elsewhere classified (kleptomania, pyromania, pathological gambling, trichotillomania)

15. Adjustment disorders (emotional difficulty resulting from an identifiable stressor)

16. Personality disorders (paranoid, schizotypal, antisocial, borderline, histrionic, narcissistic, dependent)

In what the DSM calls a **multiaxial assessment**, clients are assessed across five axes for a complete picture of their functioning. Axis 1 and 2 include the sixteen types of mental disorders listed above.

Axis 1	**Clinical disorders** and other conditions (categories 1–15)
Axis 2	**Personality disorders** (category 16) and mental retardation
Axis 3	**General medical** conditions
Axis 4	**Psychosocial** and environmental problems
Axis 5	**Global** assessment of functioning

AMERICAN PSYCHOLOGY ASSOCIATION (APA) AND PUBLICATIONS

- **The American Psychology Association (APA)** is the governing body of the field of psychology in America. It was founded in 1892 by Stanley Hall. Its purpose is to "advance psychology as a science, as a profession, and as a means of promoting human welfare."

- **American Psychologist** is the official journal of the APA. It is published monthly and includes archival, current issue, theoretical, and practical articles from all areas of psychology.

- **Psychological Bulletin** is published bimonthly by the APA and includes various papers ranging from literature reviews to quantitative reviews.

- **Psychological Abstracts,** an index published by the APA, can be found at most major libraries. It is the monthly compilation of "nonevaluative summaries of the world's literature in psychology." In each issue, the article abstracts are arranged by topic.

- The **PsycINFO** database is the online or computer access format of Psychological Abstracts. By searching for topics, authors, or titles, you can access all psychology abstracts that are catalogued under the search you chose.

For more information on the APA and all its print and online resources, go to its website: www.apa.org.

OTHER THINGS YOU SHOULD KNOW

- At least two recent tests have included one question on **primary prevention**. Primary prevention involves attempts to prevent documented psychosocial problems through direct contact with an at-risk (but thus far unaffected) group. The attempt to prevent problems is executed through proactive intervention, meaning that the intervention takes place before the problems arise rather than as a result of the problems. Examples of such primary prevention programs are prenatal health care, D.A.R.E. (Drug Abuse Resistance Education), and Head Start.

- **Culturally competent** interventions refer to treatment or prevention programs that recognize and are tailored to cultural differences. Therapists are beginning to be trained in **cultural competence**, which means that they learn the language, customs, and norms of the various cultures they serve. This minimizes Eurocentric bias and assumptions and prevents individuals from having to constantly explain their culture.

- **Community Psychology** is a model in which psychology is taken into the community via community centers or schools, as opposed to having individuals come to clinics and universities. Community Psychology emphasizes respect and also recognizes the logistics that keep the neediest people from seeking help.

> **Study Tip:** Get into a mellow routine for the whole week before the test. Studies show that your sleep (or lack of it) two or three nights before a big event has an even greater impact than your sleep the night before.

19

Measurement

DEFINED: Psychological tests are assessments of behavior, attitudes, mental constructs, personality, and mental health. Your best strategy with this section is to learn the basics of the well-known tests and to focus on the intelligence testing field.

INTELLIGENCE AND INTELLIGENCE TESTING

Intelligence is a mental construct that cannot be specifically defined. In fact, many psychologists have different ideas about what intelligence actually is. **Intelligence** is not IQ. IQ is the score one receives on an "intelligence" test. It is unlikely that IQ captures all facets of intelligence.

- **Alfred Binet** developed both the concept of the IQ and the first intelligence test **(Binet scale)**. IQ is still most commonly computed by Binet's equation: **(mental age/chronological age) × 100**. Mental age is the age level of a person's functioning according to the IQ test. The highest chronological age used in the computation is 16. After that, intelligence seems to stop developing; therefore, to use adult ages would unnecessarily decrease the IQ ratio.

Alfred Binet

- **The Mean IQ** of Americans is **100**, with a standard deviation of 15 or 16 depending on the test.

- **Stanford-Binet Intelligence Scale** is the revised version of Alfred Binet's original intelligence test. **Lewis Terman** of Stanford University was the first to revise it, hence the name. The Stanford-Binet is used with children and is organized by age level. Of all of the intelligence tests, the Stanford-Binet is the best known predictor of future academic achievement. Terman is also famous for his studies with gifted children and for the finding that children with higher IQs are better adjusted.

- **Wechsler Adult Intelligence Scale (WAIS)** is the most commonly used intelligence test for adults. Like all of the Wechsler intelligence tests, it is organized by subtests that provide subscales and identify problem areas. The version in current use is called the WAIS-III (third edition).

- **Wechsler Intelligence Scale for Children (WISC-R)** is for children aged six to sixteen.

- **Wechsler Preschool and Primary Scale of Intelligence (WPPSI)** is for children aged four to six.

- **Goodenough Draw-A-Man Test** for children is notable for its (relatively) cross-cultural application and simple directions: "Make a picture of a man. Make the very best picture that you can." Children are scored based on detail and accuracy, not artistic talent.

- **IQ correlates** most positively with IQ of biological parents (not adoptive parents) and socioeconomic status of parents (measured by either income or job-type).

- **John Horn** and **Raymond Cattell** found that **fluid intelligence** (knowing how to do something) declines with old age while **crystallized intelligence** (knowing a fact) does not.

- **Robert Zajonc** studied the relationship between birth order and intelligence. He found that first-borns were slightly more intelligent than second-borns and so on. He also found that the more children present in a family, the less intelligent they were likely to be. This relationship seems to also be affected by the spacing of the children, with greater spaces between children leading to higher intelligence.

ACADEMIC TESTS

- **Achievement tests** measure how well you know a particular subject. They measure past learning.

- **Aptitude tests** supposedly measure your innate ability to learn (but this is constantly debated). These tests are intended to predict later performance.

OBJECTIVE PERSONALITY INVENTORIES

- **Objective tests** do not allow subjects to make up their own answers, so these tests are relatively structured. **Structured tests** are often seen as more objectively scored than projective tests (see below). Most objective tests are self-reported—in other words, the subject records her own responses. However, these tests are not completely objective, because any self-report measure allows for the subject to bias her answers.

- **Q-sort** or **Q-measure** technique is the process of sorting cards into a normal distribution. Each card has a different statement on it pertaining to personality. The subject places the cards that he is neutral about at the hump of the curve. Toward one end, he places cards that he deems "very characteristic" of himself, and toward the other end, he places the "not characteristic" cards.

- **Minnesota Multiphasic Personality Inventory (MMPI)** was originally created to determine mental illness, but it is now used as a personality measure. The MMPI consists of 550 "true/false/not sure" questions. Most notably, the MMPI contains items (such as "I would like to ride a horse") that have been found to discriminate between different disorders and that subjects could not "second guess." The test has high validity primarily because it was constructed with highly discriminatory items and because it has three **validity scales** (questions that assess lying, carelessness, and faking).

- **California Personality Inventory (CPI)** is a personality measure generally used for more "normal" and less clinical groups than the MMPI. It was developed by Harrison Gough at University of California, Berkeley.

- **Julian Rotter** created the **Internal-External Locus of Control Scale** to determine whether a person feels responsible for the things that happen (internal) or that he has no control over the events in life (external).

PROJECTIVE PERSONALITY TESTS

- **Projective tests** allow the subject to create his own answer, thus facilitating the expression of conflicts, needs, and impulses. The content of the response is interpreted by the test administrator. Some projective tests are scored more objectively than others.

- **Rorschach Inkblot Test** requires that the subject describe what he sees in each of ten inkblots. Scoring is complex. The validity of the test is questionable, but its fame is not.

- **Thematic Apperception Test (TAT)** is made up of 31 cards (1 blank and 30 with pictures). The pictures show various interpersonal scenes (two people facing each other). The subject tells a story about each of the cards, which reveals aspects of her personality. The TAT is often used to measure need for achievement. **Needs, press,** and **personology** are terms that go along with interpreting the test.

- **Rosenweig Picture-Frustration (P-F) Study** consists of cartoons in which one person is frustrating another person. The subject is asked to describe how the frustrated person responds.

- **Word Association Test** was originally used in conjunction with free association techniques. A word is called out by a psychologist, and the subject says the next word to come to mind.

- **Rotter Incomplete Sentence Blank** is similar to word association. Subjects finish incomplete sentences.

- **Draw-A-Person Test** asks the subject to draw a person of each sex and to tell a story about them.

OTHER THINGS YOU SHOULD KNOW

- **Beck Depression Inventory (BDI)** is *not* used to diagnose depression. Rather, it is widely used to assess the severity of depression that has already been diagnosed. The BDI allows a therapist or researcher to follow the course of a person's depression.

- **Empirical-keying** or **criterion-keying approach** to constructing assessment instruments involves the selection of items that can discriminate between various groups. An individual's responses to the items determine if he is like a particular group or not. The **Strong-Campbell Interest Inventory** is an example of this.

- **Vocational tests** assess to what extent an individual's interests and strengths match those already found by professionals in a particular job field.

- **Lie Detector Tests** measure the arousal of the sympathetic nervous system, which becomes stimulated by lying (and anxiety).

- **Walter Mischel** was extremely critical of personality trait-theory and of personality tests in general. He felt that situations (not traits) decide actions.

- **Anne Anastasi** researched intelligence in relation to performance.

- **F-scale** or **F-ratio** is a measurement of **fascism** or **authoritarian personality**.

- **Bayley Scales of Infant Development** is not an intelligence test. It measures the sensory and motor development of infants in order to identify mentally retarded children. The Bayley scales are poor predictors of later intelligence.

Study Tip: Take a list of items you are studying to the test center. Read over these or other materials while you wait for things to get rolling. This will help your mind warm up, so that you are not still mentally asleep when the test starts. Doing this will also give you an excuse not to talk or listen to anyone else. Nervous talk won't help you.

20
Research Design

DEFINED: Research design refers to how a researcher attempts to examine a hypothesis. Different questions call for different approaches, and some approaches are more "scientific" than others.

BIG IDEAS

- A **scientific** approach to the study of psychology involves:

    - A testable hypothesis

    - A reproducible experiment that can be replicated by other scientists

    - An operationalized definition (observable and measurable) of the concept under study

- A **field study** is an experiment that takes place in a naturalistic setting. Field studies generally have much less control over the environment than laboratory experiments do. For this reason, the field generates more hypotheses than it is able to prove.

- A study adhering to **experimental design** takes place in a controlled setting (often a lab). In order to draw causal conclusions from an experiment, the researcher must be able to control certain aspects of the environment:

    - **Independent variable.** The researcher is interested in the effect of the independent variable on the dependent variable. The researcher manipulates the independent variable often by applying it in the **experimental** or **treatment condition** and by withholding it from the **control condition**.

    - **Dependent variable.** The researcher does not control the dependent variable but rather examines how the independent variable affects the dependent variable.

    - **Confounding variable.** The researcher attempts to minimize or eliminate confounding variables. These are variables in the environment that might also affect the dependent variable and would blur the effect of the independent variable on the dependent variable.

Example: A researcher is exploring the relationship between eating and sleeping. Specifically, the researcher hypothesizes that eating within an hour of going to bed causes you to sleep unsoundly. The **experimental group** will eat just before bed, but the **control group** will eat four hours before bed. All subjects will eat and sleep in the lab. The independent variable is eating before bed. The dependent variable is quality of sleep. One potential confounding variable is the possibility that simply sleeping in the lab could affect the sleep of some subjects.

DESIGN CONSIDERATIONS

Researchers are generally interested in how an independent variable affects a dependent variable in a **population** (a large group of people, such as women, college students, stockbrokers, or depressed patients). Because it is usually impossible to include all members of a population in a study, a **sample** or **subgroup** is drawn from the population. To make inferences about a population from a sample, the sample must be **representative** of the population and **unbiased**. This is most likely achieved with **random sampling.** (With this sampling procedure, every member of the population has an equal chance of being chosen for the sample.)

Other considerations:

- Particularly in developmental research, psychologists need to study people at different ages. One approach is **longitudinal design,** which involves studying the same subjects at different points in the life span. Another design is **cross-sectional**, in which different subjects of different ages are compared. This is faster and easier than longitudinal design. **Cohort-sequential** combines longitudinal and cross-sectional approaches.

- **Double-blind** experiments are those in which neither the subject nor the experimenter knows whether the subject is assigned to the treatment or to the control group.

- A **placebo** is an inactive substance or condition disguised as a treatment substance or condition. It is used to form the control group.

- **Predictive value** is the degree to which an independent variable can predict a dependent variable.

- **Generalizability** is the degree to which the results from an experiment can be applied to the population and the real world.

RESEARCH PROBLEMS

- **Acquiescence.** When people agree with opposing statements.

- **Cohort effects.** The effects that might result when a group is born and raised in a particular time period.

- **Demand characteristic.** When subjects act in ways they think the experimenter wants or expects.

- **Experimenter bias.** When researchers see what they want to see. This effect, also known as the **Rosenthal effect**, is minimized in a double-blind experiment.

- **Hawthorne effect.** When subjects alter their behavior because they are being observed. This also applies to workers altering their behavior for the same reason.

- **Nonequivalent control group.** This problematic type of control group is used when an equivalent one cannot be isolated.

- **Placebo effect.** When subjects behave differently just because they think that they have received the treatment substance or condition.

- **Reactance.** An attitude change in response to feeling that options are limited. For example, when subjects react negatively to being in an experiment by intentionally behaving unnaturally or when an individual becomes set on a certain flavor of ice cream as soon as he is told it is sold out.

- **Selective attrition.** When the subjects that drop out of an experiment are different from those that remain. The remaining sample is no longer random.

- **Social desirability bias.** When subjects do and say what they think they should.

- **Illusory correlation.** When a relationship is inferred yet when there actually is none. For example, many people insist a relationship exists between physical and personality characteristics despite evidence that no such relationship exists.

- **Meta-analysis** is a method of study that mathematically combines and summarizes the overall effects or research findings for a particular subject. Best known for consolidating various studies of the effectiveness of psychotherapy, meta-analysis can calculate one overall effect size or conclusion drawn from a collection of different studies. This method is needed when conflicting results are found and when different studies use different methods.

Study Tip: Studies have shown that the correlation between GRE scores, interview performance, and success in graduate school is illusory. None exists! So don't let these things intimidate you. Having a difficult time preparing for and applying to school does not mean that psychology grad school is not for you.

21

Statistics

DEFINED: Statistics is the process of representing or analyzing numerical data.

DESCRIPTIVE STATISTICS

Descriptive statistics organize data from a sample by showing it in a meaningful way. They do not allow conclusions to be drawn beyond the sample. The five most common forms of descriptive statistics are:

- **Percentiles** are used most commonly on standardized tests. Along with your reported score of 750, you would receive a percentile ranking of 97 percent. This shows your position in the whole group by saying that you scored higher than 97 percent of the group.

- **Frequency distributions** explain how the data in a study looked. The distributions might show how often different variables appeared. Here are some common types of variables:

  - **Nominal variables.** "Nominal" comes from the Latin word for name, so these variables are simply given descriptive names. There is no order or relationship among the variables other than to separate them into groups. Example: male, female, Republican, Democrat.

  - **Ordinal variables.** "Ordinal" implies order. Here, variables need to be arranged by order and that is it. Nothing else can be known because the variables are not necessarily equally spaced. Example: marathon finishers. A different runner comes in first, second, and third, but we do not know how far apart their finishing times were—it may have been seconds or minutes.

  - **Interval variables.** Interval variables are capable of showing order and spacing because equal spaces lie between the values. These variables, however, do not include a real zero. Example: Temperature is ordered, and the values are equally spaced. So 75 degrees is 25 degrees warmer than 50 degrees. Temperature has an arbitrary zero; however, there is no point that signifies the absence of temperature.

  - **Ratio variables.** These variables have order, equal intervals, and a real zero—they can say it all. Example: Age—after an absolute zero of not being born, age increases in equal intervals of years.

- **Graphs** are used to plot data.

  - **Frequency polygon.** This graph has plotted points connected by lines. These are often used to plot variables that are **continuous** (categories without clear boundaries).

  - **Histogram.** This graph consists of vertical bars in which the sides of the vertical bars touch. Histograms are useful for **discrete** variables that have clear boundaries and for interval variables in which there is some order. The bars are lined up in order.

- **Bar graph.** This graph is like a histogram except that the vertical bars do not touch. The various vertical columns are separated by spaces.

- **Measures of central tendency** indicate where on a number line the data set falls in general. Three types of central tendency can be calculated on a set of numbers like this one: {7, 8, 8, 9, 10, 12, 13, 13, 13}.

  - **Mean.** The mean is the same as the **average**. The mean of a set of numbers equals all of the values added together divided by the number of values. Means are highly affected by extreme scores. The mean of the above set is 10.33. **Standard error of the mean** calculates how "off" the mean might be in either direction.

  - **Median.** To find the median of a set of numbers, first line the numbers up in ascending order. Find the value that lies in the center of the row. In the above set, 10 is the number that sits dead center. If there's an even number of values in the set, take the average of the two middle values.

  - **Mode.** The mode is the most frequently occurring value. In the above set, 13 is the mode.

- **Variability** provides additional information to central tendency. It tells you how the scores are spread out overall.

  - **Range.** This most basic measure of variability simply subtracts the lowest value from the highest value in a data set. This is the overall range or **spread**.

  - **Variance** and **standard deviation** tell us how much variation there is among n number of scores in a distribution. To calculate variance, you figure out how much each score differs (or deviates) from the mean by subtracting the mean from each score. Then you must square each of these deviation values (this gets rid of negative values that result when scores fall below the mean). Now you add all these squared deviations to get the sum of the squares. Now divide this sum by the number of scores you had in the first place, by n—this gives you the variance in a sample. But remember that all of these values were squared, so to find the average deviation, or standard deviation, from the mean you take the square root of the variance. Standard deviation tells you the average extent to which scores were different from the mean. If the average standard deviation is large, then scores were highly dispersed. If the standard deviation is small, then scores were very close together. Different standard distributions make it difficult to compare scores on two different tests.

THE NORMAL DISTRIBUTION

The **normal distribution**, also known as the **bell curve**, is quite important. In an ideal world, scores such as those for the GRE are intended to look like a bell curve. The larger your sample, the greater your chance of having a normal distribution of values. Here's what you should know about the normal distribution:

- It is **unimodal**—it has only one hump. The majority of scores fall in the middle ranges. There are fewer scores at the extremes.

- **Z-scores** refer to how many standard deviations a score is from the mean. For practical purposes, z-scores of normal distributions range from -3 to +3, because this covers the vast majority of scores on a normal curve.

- To combat problems of comparing scores and distributions of scores with different standard deviations, normal distributions can be standardized. These are known as standard normal distributions. The standard normal distribution is the same thing as a normal distribution, but it has been standardized so that the mean for every such distribution is 0 and the standard deviation is 1. **Standard normal distributions** and z-scores allow you to compare one person's scores on two different distributions. For example, if a person's intelligence matches his or her achievement on the GRE Psychology Test, you would expect someone to receive the same z-score on an IQ test and on the GRE Pyschology test (e.g., a z-score of +2), even though both tests use two different scoring systems. This would mean that the person's score should be 2 standard deviations above the mean in both cases. If we saw that the person's IQ score was 130, or two standard deviations above the mean, giving a z-score of +2, and his or her GRE subject test score was 570, or right at the mean, giving a z-score of 0, we would hypothesize that for some reason this individual was not performing to his or her potential.

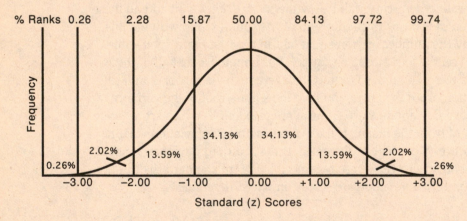

The Standard Normal Distribution

Cumulative Percentile Distribution	
% score	cum % rank
+3.00	99.74
+2.00	97.72
+1.00	84.13
0.00	50.00
−1.00	15.87
−2.00	2.28
−3.00	0.26

- Know all the numbers on the standard normal distribution and how they map onto a normal distribution. For example, if John scores an 88 in a test in which the mean is 80 and the standard deviation is 4, then on a normal distribution of scores in the class John's score would lie two standard deviations above the mean. If this normal distribution of scores were then standardized to have a mean of 0 and a standard deviation of 1, then John's score of 88 would now be meaningless—what we would know instead is that he had a z-score of 2. We would also know that John lies in the 97th percentile meaning that 97% of students score lower than he did.

- It is important to be able to reproduce the standard normal distribution and all of the numbers that go with it so that you can evaluate problems similar to the one above. Know what z-scores go with what percentile ranks. And know the percentage of scores that lie in each area; for example, know that 68% of scores lie within one standard deviation (in either direction) of the mean. To make this easy, learn this ratio 34:14:2 and know that it applies to both sides of the mean.

Not all distributions are normal. Learn the names of the other types:

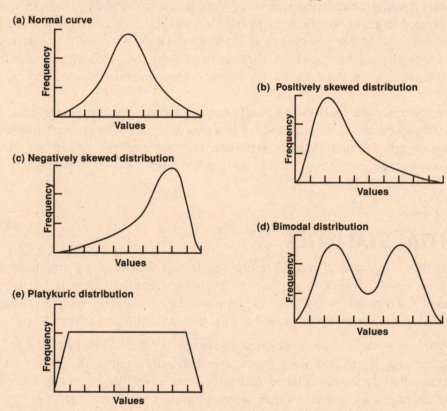

Examples of frequency distributions found in behavioral science research

CORRELATIONAL STATISTICS

Correlations are part of statistics but are neither purely descriptive nor purely inferential. Correlations can only show **relationships** (NOT causality) between variables. The different types of correlations or relationships are:

- **Positive.** A positive correlation is simple and linear. As one variable increases so does the other. Example: Food intake and weight are positively correlated; the more you eat, the more you weigh.

- **Negative.** A negative correlation is simple and linear. As one variable goes up, the other goes down. Example: Exercise and weight. With other factors held constant, as the amount you exercise increases, the amount you weigh decreases.

- **Curvilinear.** A curvilinear relationship is not simple and linear. It looks like a curved line. Example: Arousal and performance. Low arousal and high arousal lead to poor performance, but a medium amount of arousal leads to successful performance.

- **Zero correlation.** This is no relationship.

The **Pearson r correlation coefficient** is a way of numerically calculating and expressing correlation. You don't need to know how to find a Pearson's r, but you do need to know what the r values mean. The Pearson r values range from -1 to $+1$. A value of -1 indicates a perfect negative correlation. A value of $+1$ indicates a perfect positive correlation. A value of 0 indicates no relationship. The strength of the relationship is indicated by how far away the value is from zero and how close it is to -1 or $+1$.

A **Spearman r correlation coefficient** is another correlation used only when the data is in the form of ranks. It is the procedure for determining the line that describes a linear relationship. **Regression** is the step beyond simple correlations. A **statistical regression** allows you to not only identify a relationship between two variables but also to make predictions about one variable based on another variable.

INFERENTIAL STATISTICS

Inferential statistics allow you to generalize findings from a sample to a population, which is the larger group from which the sample was drawn. **Statistics** refer to numbers that describe a sample, and **parameters** refer to numbers that describe populations. We use statistics to estimate population parameters. That is, we use statistics to predict or estimate what happens outside the sample.

- When a researcher uses a statistical test (whatever it may be), he or she is usually hoping to find that the sample statistics are **significant**. This means that the numbers that describe the sample (e.g., that men are taller on average than women, or that treatment groups in therapy trials perform better than control groups) are describing a real difference or pattern rather than just random variation. If findings are statistically significant, then researchers can **generalize** these same findings to the population.

- When a researcher uses a **test of significance** he or she is hoping to **reject the null hypothesis**, which is the hypothesis that no real differences or patterns exist. If a test of significance shows that results were statistically significant (not likely caused by chance), then the null hypothesis is rejected.

- Researchers cannot always know for certain whether their findings are correct, but certain standards are accepted. Most researchers use a significance level, also known as **alpha** level, of <.05 or <.01. This means that the chance that seemingly significant errors are due to random variation rather than to true, systematic variance is less than 5/100 or less than 1/100, respectively.

- **Type I errors** occur when you incorrectly reject the null hypothesis—that is, you thought your findings were significant but they were really only caused by chance. **Type II errors** are when you wrongly accept the null hypothesis—in other words, tests showed your findings to be insignificant when in fact they were significant.

Which tests of significance you use depends on the characteristics of your sample and of your dependent variable. The most commonly used tests of significance are the following:

- **T-tests** compare the **means of two different groups** to see if the two groups are truly different. This would mean that the difference between the means is large enough to be considered statistically significant rather than due to chance variation. T-tests analyze differences between means on **continuous data** (anything that is measured such as height or depression score on a depression scale as opposed to things that are counted such as group size, number of hospital visits, number of symptoms; which is discrete data) and are particularly useful with samples that have small "n" (meaning few subjects). T-tests cannot test for differences between more than two groups.

- **Chi-square** tests are used when the n-cases in a sample are classified into categories or **cells**. The results of the chi-square test tell us whether the **groups are significantly different in size**. Chi-squares look at patterns or distributions (not differences between means). For example, imagine that 100 members of an Introduction to Psychology class are categorized based on race (Caucasian, African-American, Asian-American, Hispanic, Native American). Insignificant results of a chi-square test of this data would tell us that no one race tended to be enrolled in Introduction to Psychology significantly more than any other race. Chi-square tests analyze **categorical** or **discrete** data (data that has been counted rather than measured and so is usually limited to positive and whole values) and can be used on small samples. Chi-square tests can also assess the "goodness of fit" of distributions or whether the pattern is what would be expected.

- **ANOVA** or **analysis of variance** is a highly utilized test because of its flexibility. It is similar to the t-test in that it analyzes the **differences among means** of continuous variables but it is more flexible than the t-test because it can analyze the difference among more than two groups (even if the groups have different sample sizes). **One-Way ANOVA** simply tests whether the means on one outcome or dependent variable (e.g., height or level of anxiety from an anxiety scale) are significantly different across groups. **Two-Way ANOVA** can test the effects of two independent variables or treatment conditions at once.

- **Factorial analysis of variance** is used when an experiment involves more than one independent variable. This analysis can separate the effects of different levels of different variables. Example: If you were studying the effect of brain lesions on problem solving, you could have two independent variables (lesion and type of problem) and one dependent variable (success with problem). Give each independent variable two levels apiece (with and without lesions, simple and complex tasks). This is a 2 × 2 design, which would yield four different combinations for evaluation.

A factor analysis can isolate the **main effects** (the effect of lesions on problem solving and the effect of type of task on problem solving). More importantly, a factor analysis can identify **interaction effects**. Here, you can combine the independent variables. (Do people with lesions do better on simple tasks than people without lesions do on complex tasks?)

- **Analysis of Covariance (ANCOVA)** tests whether at least two groups co-vary. Importantly, the ANCOVA can adjust for pre-existing differences between groups.

- **Linear Regression** allows you to use correlation coefficients in order to predict one variable y from another variable x. Correlations measure the linear relationship between two variables, but they do not describe the relationship. For example, we might know that the correlation between extraversion and the number of friends you have is .73; but this does not let us predict from an extraversion score how many friends someone would probably have. Linear regression allows us to define a line on a graph that describes the relationship between x and y. In general, the same data you used to calculate a correlation is now plotted onto a graph.

Let's use extraversion score as our *x*-variable and number of friends as our *y*-variable. Imagine a graph with extraversion on the *x*-axis and friends on the *y*-axis. The dots on the graph are the data from the individual subjects. Linear regression is when the **least-squares line** or **regression line** is fit to the data. This line would be situated so that the distance between each point of data and the line is as small as possible (this is determined by finding the difference between each data point and the line, squaring these differences to get rid of negative values, and then summing them). Fortunately, computer programs do this for you, and it will not be required on the GRE test. Just know that regressions use correlational data to make predictions based on a line fit with the least-squares method.

CREATING MEASURES

Statistics are an important part of creating new tests or measures. They ensure that the measures are on target.

- Tests are **standardized** (or tried out on huge groups of people) in order to create norms.

- **Criterion-referenced tests** measure mastery in a particular area or subject (the final exam of a course, for example).

- **Domain-referenced tests** attempt to measure less defined properties (like intelligence) and need to be checked for reliability and validity.

- **Reliability** means how stable the measure is:

    - **Test-retest reliability** is measured by the same individual taking the same test more than once. On a test with high test-retest reliability, that person would get approximately the same score each time.

    - **Split-half reliability** is measured by comparing an individual's performance on two halves of the same test (odd vs. even questions for example). This reveals the **internal consistency** of a test. Another way to increase internal consistency of a measure is to perform an **item analysis**, analyzing how a large group responded to each item on the measure. This process weeds out dud or problematic questions so they can be replaced with better questions (ones with discriminatory value). This increases internal consistency.

- **Validity** means how well the test measures a construct:

- **Internal validity** measures the extent to which the different items within a measure "hang together" and test the same thing.

- **External validity** is the extent to which a test measures what it intends to measure. There are four aspects of external validity:

  1. **Concurrent validity** is whether scores on a new measure positively correlate with other measures known to test the same construct. This process is **cross validation**.

  2. **Construct validity** is whether the test really taps the abstract concept being measured.

  3. **Content validity** is whether the content of the test covers a good sample of the construct being measured (not just part of it).

  4. **Face validity** is whether the test items simply look like they measure the construct.

  5. **Donald Campbell** and **Donald Fiske** created the **multitrait-multimethod technique** to determine the validity of tests.

PART **III**

The Princeton Review Practice GRE Psychology Subject Test

22

Practice Test

Psychology Test
Time–170 Minutes
215 Questions

Directions: Each of the questions or incomplete statements below is followed by five suggested answers or completions. Select the one that is best in each case and then completely fill in the corresponding space on the answer sheet.

1. A child with an IQ of 63 would most likely be diagnosed with

    (A) mild mental retardation
    (B) severe mental retardation
    (C) profound mental retardation
    (D) moderate mental retardation
    (E) borderline mental retardation

2. A phenomenological view of personality asserts that type theory neglects the

    (A) superego
    (B) self
    (C) supernatural
    (D) proprium
    (E) id

3. Which of the following is one of the sixteen major diagnostic categories used in the DSM-IV?

    (A) borderline disorders
    (B) paranoid disorders
    (C) obsessive-compulsive disorders
    (D) factitious disorders
    (E) panic disorders

4. What is the key distinction between classical conditioning and operant conditioning?

    (A) Operant conditioning attempts to pair an unrelated stimulus and response, whereas classical conditioning attempts to extinguish such pairings.
    (B) Operant conditioning focuses on rewards, whereas classical conditioning focuses on punishment.
    (C) Operant conditioning attempts to pair an unrelated stimulus and response, whereas classical conditioning underscores the consequences of behavior.
    (D) Operant conditioning emphasizes the consequences of behavior, whereas classical conditioning emphasizes the association between stimuli.
    (E) Operant conditioning is used in human therapy, whereas classical conditioning is used only with other animals.

5. A child in Piaget's preoperational stage is given a toy and attempts to eat it. This child is demonstrating

    (A) generalization
    (B) accommodation
    (C) assimilation
    (D) transition
    (E) overextension

6. Which of the following is NOT true of systematic desensitization?

    (A) The technique is attributed to Joseph Wolpe.
    (B) It is a highly effective treatment for phobias.
    (C) It employs counter-conditioning principles.
    (D) It reduces anxiety.
    (E) It employs operant conditioning.

7. If the GRE Psychology Subject Test had a standard error of zero, then a test-taker that took the test two times would necessarily receive

(A) a score equivalent to a z-score of 1 each time
(B) the same score on each test
(C) two scores that correlated perfectly with the test-taker's aptitude
(D) two scores that were above the mean
(E) two perfect scores

8. Deutsch used the "prisoner's dilemma" to study what social phenomenon?

(A) conformity v. reactance
(B) attribution
(C) cooperation v. competition
(D) stereotypes
(E) bias

9. A brooding herring gull is presented with various eggs of differing size and coloration. She can only incubate one. The egg that she chooses will most likely be

(A) closest to her nest
(B) an exact replica of a herring gull egg
(C) a supernormal sign stimulus
(D) extremely small in size
(E) not colored

10. Noam Chomsky posited that humans have a unique, inborn ability to understand the structure of language and to apply this to language learning. Chomsky called this the

(A) innate surface structure ability
(B) innate capability index
(C) prosody index
(D) language acquisition device
(E) collective endowment device

11. Two major dimensions of personality hypothesized by Hans Eysenck are

(A) stability and introversion
(B) masculinity and femininity
(C) stability and masculinity
(D) internal control and external control
(E) extraversion and repression

12. According to Erik Erikson, a young adult would be most concerned with which of the following issues?

(A) identity
(B) sex-typed behavior
(C) autonomy
(D) achievement
(E) intimacy

GO ON TO THE NEXT PAGE.

13. The victim of a car accident has no physiological feeling in his body. He can,
however, think and speak. The man notices
that since the injury, his emotions have been
practically nonexistent. This situation
supports which theory of emotion?

(A) James-Lange theory
(B) Cannon-Bard theory
(C) Sperry theory
(D) Post-Traumatic Stress theory
(E) Metacognitive theory

14. Among the following tests, which one is the
best predictor of academic achievement?

(A) Bayley Scales of Infant Development
(B) the WISC-R
(C) the WPPSI
(D) the WAIS
(E) the Stanford-Binet Intelligence Scale

15. Hazel has experienced feelings of worthlessness, low energy, and a loss of interest in
life for most of the days of the past three
years. She would most likely be diagnosed
with

(A) major depressive disorder
(B) dysthymic disorder
(C) severe melancholia
(D) existential neurosis
(E) bipolar disorder

16. The Strange Situation is used in order to
study

(A) infant attachment
(B) Hawthorne effect
(C) groupthink
(D) diffusion of responsibility
(E) Barnum effect

17. Which of the following activities best serves
to hold information in short-term memory?

(A) clustering
(B) chunking
(C) rehearsing
(D) attending
(E) associating

18. Which of the following is NOT characteristic of stage 1 sleep?

(A) dreams
(B) REM
(C) desynchronized EEG patterns
(D) major muscle twitches
(E) difficulty being roused

19. The DSM-IV presents a scheme for assessment called multiaxial assessment. It is called multiaxial because it employs five different axes for evaluation in order to create a complete picture of the client. Which of the following is NOT one of the five axes used?

    (A) dreams
    (B) general medical conditions
    (C) psychosocial problems
    (D) personality disorders
    (E) clinical disorders

Questions 20 and 21 apply to the research study described below:

A researcher wants to consider the effects of preparation on standardized test scores. She plans to compare the GRE scores of students who did and did not take a preparation course for the GRE. She also plans to compare the GRE scores of students who took preparation courses through Company X, Company Y, and Company Z.

20. Which of the following statistical tests should the researcher use to analyze her data?

    (A) Pearson's r correlation coefficient
    (B) t-test
    (C) chi-square test
    (D) 2 x 2 x 2 factor analysis
    (E) 2 x 3 factor analysis

21. The researcher found that students who took a preparation course with Companies X and Y scored higher on the GRE than students who did not prepare. But students who took a preparation course with Company Z scored no higher on average than students who did not take a preparation course. This result is an example of

    (A) a negative correlation
    (B) a zero correlation
    (C) an interaction effect
    (D) a main effect
    (E) a flat effect

22. Androgyny as an area of study is most associated with which of the following?

    (A) Karen Horney
    (B) Sandra Bem
    (C) Eleanor Maccoby
    (D) Matina Horner
    (E) Diana Baumrind

23. Social comparison theory has been used as an argument against

    (A) deindividuation
    (B) group polarization
    (C) single-sex schools
    (D) segregation
    (E) mainstreaming in schools

24. Which of the following phenomena is minimized by a group monitoring?

    (A) social loafing
    (B) social comparison
    (C) ingroup/outgroup bias
    (D) groupthink
    (E) group polarization

GO ON TO THE NEXT PAGE.

25. A two year old who wants to be handed a ball might simply say "ball." This is an example of

(A) holophrastic speech
(B) telegraphic speech
(C) overregulated speech
(D) overextended speech
(E) neologistic speech

26. After moving into a home very near to a hospital, a young child became frightened and upset each time he heard ambulance sirens racing by. With time, the child seemed less bothered by the sirens. Eventually, the child seemed not to notice the sirens at all. This lessened reaction to the sirens is most likely caused by

(A) chaining
(B) habituation
(C) extinction
(D) sensitization
(E) shaping

27. Which of the following methods is most commonly used to study selective attention?

(A) shadowing in a dichotic listening task
(B) presentation of subliminal messages on a screen
(C) presentation of subliminal messages on a audiotape
(D) presentation of two stimuli separated by one just noticeable difference
(E) questionnaires that test the contents of short-term memory

28. Bottom-up information processing is best described as

(A) semantically driven
(B) phonetically driven
(C) schematically driven
(D) morphologically driven
(E) data driven

29. Kohlberg devised his theory of moral development through the use of

(A) observations of individual action in contrived moral dilemmas
(B) naturalistic observations of children
(C) themes in mythology
(D) verbal responses to hypothetical moral dilemmas
(E) objective personality inventories

30. Long-term use of a dopamine blocking neuroleptic would probably improve the condition of

(A) tardive dyskinesia
(B) Parkinson's disease
(C) schizophrenia
(D) both schizophrenia and Parkinson's disease
(E) Wernicke's syndrome

31. Which of the following figures is credited with founding the first laboratory dedicated to psychology?

    (A) Johannes Müller
    (B) Thomas Harvey
    (C) Sigmund Freud
    (D) Gustav Fechner
    (E) Wilhelm Wundt

32. Which of the following statements is true of maintenance rehearsal?

    (A) Maintenance rehearsal keeps material in short-term memory.
    (B) Maintenance rehearsal keeps material in long-term memory.
    (C) Maintenance rehearsal transfers material to long-term memory.
    (D) Maintenance rehearsal is also called secondary rehearsal.
    (E) Maintenance rehearsal uses elaboration.

33. In many jury trials, defense lawyers use the strategy of blaming the victim, so that the accused perpetrator might be set free. People's tendency to go along with victim blaming can be explained by

    (A) oversimplification
    (B) the representativeness heuristic
    (C) the just world bias
    (D) the illusion of control
    (E) the illusory correlation

34. Which of the following is NOT a morpheme?

    (A) the suffix "-ed"
    (B) the vowel combination "ee"
    (C) the word "cat"
    (D) the suffix "s"
    (E) the prefix "anti-"

35. A neuron in the brain has recently fired. The neuron completes its absolute refractory period and then is in the relative refractory period. At this point, the neuron is stimulated by a stronger stimulus, and it fires again. Which of the following is true of that neuron?

    (A) It is hyperpolarized.
    (B) The action potential will not be completed because of the refractory period.
    (C) The second action potential will be of greater intensity than the first.
    (D) The second action potential will be of the same intensity as the first.
    (E) The second action potential will be of lesser intensity than the first.

36. In the criterion-keying or empirical-keying approach to test construction, the researcher

    (A) must include items which allow for projective answers
    (B) must include items which could produce percentile ranks
    (C) must include items which allow for a range of scores
    (D) must include items which discriminate between groups
    (E) must include items which measure speed

GO ON TO THE NEXT PAGE.

37. According to Piaget, an individual in which of the following stages might demonstrate circular reactions?

(A) accommodational
(B) sensorimotor
(C) preoperational
(D) concrete operational
(E) formal operational

38. The theory that a child steals candy because he is a thief is an example of a

(A) availability heuristic
(B) cognitive bias
(C) dispositional attribution
(D) response set
(E) situational attribution

39. Fritz Heider is known as the founder of

(A) attribution theory
(B) social psychology
(C) self-perception theory
(D) personality psychology
(E) social facilitation theory

40. A manager of an advertising company is encouraging her workers to think "outside the box" in order to come up with entirely new angles for advertising. In essence, the manager is asking her employees to think

(A) metacognitively
(B) convergently
(C) fluidly
(D) deductively
(E) divergently

41. A pigeon is placed in a "Skinner box" which is outfitted with a key for pecking and a chute that delivers food. Through shaping, the experimenter plans to condition the bird to peck the key in order to obtain food. The experimenter will need to use

(A) secondary reinforcement
(B) autonomic conditioning
(C) differential reinforcement
(D) autoshaping
(E) trace conditioning

42. Humans see better at night by looking at objects from the side than by looking straight at objects. This is explained by

(A) the opponent-process theory
(B) the way rods are distributed on the retina
(C) the tri-color theory
(D) lateral geniculate activity
(E) the crossing of the optic nerves in the neural pathway

43. According to Craik and Lockhart, which of the following levels of processing would result in the highest recall of information?

   (A) phonological
   (B) syntactic
   (C) repetitive
   (D) acoustic
   (E) semantic

44. Which of the following researchers used factor analysis to identify personality source traits?

   (A) Charles Spearman
   (B) Walter Mischel
   (C) Gordon Allport
   (D) Raymond Cattell
   (E) George Kelley

Questions 45 and 46 are based on the following experiment:

In a laboratory experiment, subjects wear headphones and are tested individually. Each of 500 subjects is presented first with a light and then possibly with a low-intensity tone in the earphones. Subjects are instructed to push a button if they hear a tone. Subjects are rewarded with $10 for each hit. In 500 trials, 200 times a tone was presented, and 300 times a tone was not presented. One hundred and ninety tones were detected. Also, the button was pressed 270 times in response to no tone.

45. Which of the following describes the subjects' overall performance?

   (A) 10 misses and 30 false alarms
   (B) 10 misses and 30 correct rejections
   (C) 460 hits
   (D) 190 hits and 270 misses
   (E) 280 misses

46. Which of the following statements about the above experiment is in line with signal detection theory?

   (A) The reward offered for hits increased subjects' overall response accuracy.
   (B) Subjects were unable to detect at least a few tones because some tones were not a just noticeable difference from the previously presented tones.
   (C) The reward for hits probably caused the high number of false alarms.
   (D) Some subjects might have been distracted by the experiment design which called on visual and auditory sensory systems.
   (E) The tone and the light were probably not effectively paired because the tone only followed the light in 200 of the 500 trials.

GO ON TO THE NEXT PAGE.

47. According to Kohlberg, an individual in a stage of conventional morality would be most concerned with

(A) gaining rewards
(B) gaining approval
(C) avoiding punishment
(D) achieving fairness
(E) adhering to the conservative point of view

48. Which of the following areas in the brain has been shown in experiments to be closely connected to hunger, eating, and satiation?

(A) medulla oblongata
(B) hippocampus
(C) hypothalamus
(D) thalamus
(E) corpus callosum

49. Which of the following is characteristic of psychosis?

(A) the propensity for violence
(B) the absence of logic
(C) the presence of erroneous beliefs and/or hallucinations
(D) more than one personality
(E) motor tics

50. Kenneth and Mamie Clark's doll preference studies were used

(A) to elicit accounts of childhood sexual abuse
(B) to demonstrate regression in adults
(C) to demonstrate gender favoritism in the classroom
(D) as evidence in *Brown v. The Board of Education*
(E) as evidence in the Kitty Genovese case

51. To motivate himself to study, a student decides that after learning a chapter of material he will treat himself to a movie. In this situation, seeing a movie is acting as a reinforcement for studying. This situation demonstrates

(A) the Premack principle
(B) a fixed-interval ratio schedule
(C) autoshaping
(D) the Garcia effect
(E) higher-order conditioning

52. The view that the mind is a "tabula rasa" at birth and written on by experience is most commonly associated with

(A) Edward Thorndike
(B) Immanuel Kant
(C) John Locke
(D) René Descartes
(E) Thomas Hobbes

53. An experimenter wants to train a dog to bark at a red light. The dog naturally barks at a mouse when it is presented outside the dog's cage. For countless trials, the experimenter presents the mouse and then the red light. The dog never learns to bark at the red light because

(A) the UCS and the CS are not at all similar
(B) the UCS and the CS are presented in the wrong order
(C) the UCR and the CS are not at all similar
(D) the CS is not salient enough
(E) the CS precedes the UCS

54. According to Roger Brown and other psycholinguistic researchers, children refine the way they apply grammatical rules through

(A) positive reinforcement from caregivers
(B) positive conditioning from caregivers
(C) experience and self-correction
(D) memorization of what others say
(E) structured learning

55. According to Freud's developmental theory, a child who is particularly frustrated during a stage of development is like to experience

(A) fixation
(B) identification
(C) castration anxiety if a boy
(D) overdevelopment of the superego
(E) ego anxiety

56. Which of the following explains why cartoons are not perceived as a series of still frames?

(A) autokinetic effect
(B) motion parallax
(C) the Ponzo illusion
(D) the Müller-Lyer illusion
(E) the Phi phenomenon

57. Which of the following disorders was formerly known as dementia praecox?

(A) Alzheimer's
(B) Parkinson's
(C) Huntington's chorea
(D) Multiple personality disorder
(E) Schizophrenia

58. Visual acuity is highest under what circumstances?

(A) when the cones in the periphery of the retina are stimulated
(B) when the rods on the fovea are stimulated
(C) when the rods and the cones are equally stimulated
(D) when the cones on the fovea are stimulated
(E) when the rods in the periphery of the retina are stimulated

GO ON TO THE NEXT PAGE.

59. In research on attachment, Harlow placed infant rhesus monkeys with "surrogate mothers." In this famous experiment, a stimulus that induced fear in the infant would cause the infant to run to

(A) the adult female who most resembled its biological mother
(B) the closest object behind which it could hide
(C) the surrogate with the bottle
(D) the surrogate covered with terrycloth
(E) none of the above, as it knew none were its biological mother

60. A therapist listens to the choices of his client with unconditional positive regard. The goal of this therapy is most likely

(A) a sense of meaningfulness
(B) congruence for the self
(C) complete awareness of the here and now
(D) decreased inferiority
(E) development of effective beliefs

61. Erikson's developmental theory centered around

(A) biological forces
(B) cognitive changes
(C) moral development
(D) psychosocial crises
(E) need development

62. The most common way of studying human cognitive processing is to evaluate

(A) semantic shifts
(B) EEG readings
(C) reaction time
(D) rehearsal time
(E) creativity

63. Because Shay is a good student, her teacher assumes she is also artistic, well behaved, and from a good family. The teacher's assumptions are explained by

(A) the halo effect
(B) oversimplification
(C) good continuation
(D) self-fulfilling prophecy
(E) self-serving bias

64. Trait theory in personality has been most criticized for

(A) having contradictory dimensions
(B) attempting to quantify the impossible
(C) not identifying one agreed-upon dimension of personality
(D) not addressing heredity
(E) assuming that people behave consistently in various situations

65. Which of the following is NOT a maladaptive cognition according to cognitive therapy?

    (A) dichotomous thinking
    (B) personalizing
    (C) denying
    (D) overgeneralizing
    (E) magnifying

66. Which of the following figures suggested the dual code hypothesis in relation to facilitating recall?

    (A) Karl Lashley
    (B) Allan Paivio
    (C) Fergus Craik
    (D) Thomas Harvey
    (E) Hermann Ebbinghaus

67. Which of the following reflexes might be elicited by stroking the bottom of a baby's foot?

    (A) Neo-ped reflex
    (B) Moro reflex
    (C) Babinski reflex
    (D) Palmar reflex
    (E) Kleinfetter reflex

68. The part of the brain that is connected to the very basic function of simple alertness is the

    (A) superior colliculus
    (B) inferior colliculus
    (C) medulla oblongata
    (D) reticular formation
    (E) hippocampus

69. Which of the following disorders is the modern name for hysteria?

    (A) paresis
    (B) hypochondriasis
    (C) conversion disorder
    (D) factitious disorder
    (E) narcissistic personality

Questions 70 and 71 refer to the following:

Tom's favorite hobby has always been skiing. Recently, Tom took a job in which he is paid a large sum of money to patrol the ski slopes daily.

70. According to Daryl Bem, Tom's attitude about skiing

    (A) will remain unchanged
    (B) will become more negative
    (C) will become more positive
    (D) will vacillate because of cognitive dissonance
    (E) will be negative only on days when he is not paid to ski

71. The change in Tom's attitude, according to self-perception theory, would result from

    (A) self-fulfilling prophecy
    (B) overjustification
    (C) mere-exposure effect
    (D) innoculation
    (E) gain-loss theory

GO ON TO THE NEXT PAGE.

72. Which of the following would be most inclined toward a situational view of personality?

    (A) Walter Mischel
    (B) Raymond Cattell
    (C) Gordon Allport
    (D) Hans Eysenck
    (E) William Sheldon

73. The APA was founded by

    (A) John Watson
    (B) William James
    (C) Stanley Hall
    (D) Wilhelm Wundt
    (E) B.F. Skinner

74. Who wrote *Civilization and Its Discontents*?

    (A) René Descartes
    (B) Carl Jung
    (C) Jean Piaget
    (D) Kurt Koffka
    (E) Sigmund Freud

75. Weber's law applies to a specific range of intensities in

    (A) hearing only
    (B) vision only
    (C) hearing and vision only
    (D) all of the senses
    (E) none of the senses because it has been disproved

76. While swimming in the ocean, a woman was stung by several jellyfish. Now the woman refuses to swim at all, even at an indoor pool. Her new fear of swimming can be attributed to

    (A) operant conditioning
    (B) trace conditioning
    (C) delayed conditioning
    (D) second-order conditioning
    (E) classical conditioning

77. Which of the following is true of a variable-ratio schedule of reinforcement as opposed to other schedules of reinforcement?

    (A) It provides a reinforcement for any response.
    (B) Of the various reinforcement schedules, it causes learning to occur the fastest.
    (C) It explains why people wait endlessly for a late bus.
    (D) It is extremely vulnerable to extinction.
    (E) It produces the highest rate of responding.

78. A normal distribution of 2000 scores has a mean of 150 and a standard deviation of 6. Jenny received a 162. Each of the following is true of her score EXCEPT

    (A) approximately 68% of students scored lower than she did
    (B) approximately 48% of the total scores lie between her score and the mean
    (C) her score is two standard deviations from the mean
    (D) her score is equivalent to a z-score of +2
    (E) her percentile rank is approximately the 98th percentile

79. An individual sternly gives orders in his own home and obediently follows orders at work. This person might score particularly high on the

(A) Rotter Locus of Control Scale
(B) TAT
(C) CPI
(D) F-scale
(E) Bem Sex Role Inventory

80. The receptors for hearing are located on which of the following in humans?

(A) olivary nucleus
(B) inferior colliculus
(C) oval window
(D) tympanic membrane
(E) basilar membrane

81. According to Piaget, a child that recognizes that a round ball of clay maintains its mass even when flattened into a long thin cylinder must have acquired which cognitive skill?

(A) object permanence
(B) transmutation
(C) generalization
(D) conservation
(E) transformation

82. Gibson and Walk developed a famous apparatus to study

(A) selective attention
(B) coordination
(C) subliminal perception
(D) peripheral vision
(E) depth perception

83. Which of the following personality disorders is characterized by excessive emotion and attention seeking?

(A) histrionic
(B) antisocial
(C) dependent
(D) schizotypal
(E) borderline

84. An IQ of 146 is approximately how many standard deviations from the mean?

(A) 5
(B) 4
(C) 3
(D) 2
(E) 1

GO ON TO THE NEXT PAGE.

85. The fundamental attribution error is the tendency to

   (A) attribute every behavior to some motive
   (B) personify inanimate objects
   (C) project personal motivations onto the behaviors of others
   (D) attribute one's own mistakes to disposition
   (E) attribute the behaviors of others to disposition

86. On the GRE, a student would answer a question about Erikson more quickly if it were preceded by another question about Erikson than if it were preceded by a question about physiological psychology. This effect is due to

   (A) atmosphere effect
   (B) semantic priming
   (C) chunking
   (D) top-down processing
   (E) acoustic effect

87. An individual with Korsakoff's syndrome might engage in

   (A) neologisms
   (B) echolalia
   (C) echopraxia
   (D) confabulations
   (E) folie a deux

88. Gordon Allport is known for what type of approach to understanding personality?

   (A) personal construct
   (B) nomothetic
   (C) ideographic
   (D) factor analysis
   (E) phrenologic

89. According to Piaget, an individual who entertains himself by solving logic puzzles must be in which of the following cognitive stages?

   (A) accommodational
   (B) sensorimotor
   (C) preoperational
   (D) concrete operational
   (E) formal operational

90. Which of the following therapies would most appropriate for an individual who suffered from strong feelings of meaninglessness and who hoped to find more meaning in life?

   (A) Client-centered therapy
   (B) Psychoanalytic therapy
   (C) Existential therapy
   (D) Individual therapy
   (E) Gestalt therapy

91. Which of the following brain areas is important for speech?

    (A) right cerebral hemisphere
    (B) cerebellum
    (C) thalamus
    (D) hippocampus
    (E) Wernicke's area

92. E. L. Thorndike is known for each of the following EXCEPT

    (A) the law of effect
    (B) the concept of instrumental learning
    (C) the discovery of state-dependent learning
    (D) learning experiments using cats in puzzle boxes
    (E) asserting that individuals repeat behaviors that lead to positive consequences

93. In a territory that is inhabited by many similar looking and closely related bird species, a male bird performs an elaborate display prior to mating. The display ensures that the female partner will be of the same species as the male. This is an example of

    (A) a behavioral isolating mechanism
    (B) a fixed action pattern
    (C) paternal behavior
    (D) habituation
    (E) exploratory behavior

94. Which of the following theorists has been recognized for creating a developmental theory that covers the entire life span?

    (A) Abraham Maslow
    (B) Lawrence Kohlberg
    (C) Erik Erikson
    (D) Jean Piaget
    (E) Sigmund Freud

95. The Kitty Genovese case sparked research into

    (A) vicarious behavior
    (B) the glass ceiling
    (C) racial segregation
    (D) the bystander effect
    (E) violence against women

96. In research on social learning theory, Bandura conducted the famous Bobo doll experiment. Based on this experiment, what did Bandura conclude was important to social learning in children?

    (A) observational learning
    (B) primary reinforcement
    (C) rewards
    (D) concept learning
    (E) shaping

GO ON TO THE NEXT PAGE.

97. Watson would expect which of the following factors to most influence child behavioral development?

(A) morality
(B) imitation
(C) psychodynamic influences
(D) pyschosocial factors
(E) exploration needs

98. According to Collins and Quillian, to which of the following statements would subjects take the longer amount of time to answer "true?"

(A) A shoe is a piece of clothing.
(B) A ballet slipper is a shoe.
(C) A boot is a shoe.
(D) A sandal is a piece of clothing.
(E) A sandal is a shoe.

99. Which is true of the ossicles in the auditory system?

(A) The stapes tap against the oval window.
(B) The stapes tap against the tympanic membrane.
(C) Their movement is known as the traveling wave.
(D) They are located in the inner ear.
(E) They are located in the outer ear.

100. Which of the following types of tests is paired correctly with its form of memory testing?

(A) essay test....cued recall
(B) language test....recognition
(C) fill-in-the-blank test....cued recall
(D) multiple-choice test....cued recall
(E) sentence completion test....recognition

101. Upon spotting a predator, a hidden bird makes a call of alarm. This display of altruism now places the hidden bird at increased risk while placing its nearby siblings at decreased risk. Such an act is best explained by the concept of

(A) contact comfort behavior
(B) operant behavior
(C) natural selection
(D) irrelevant behavior
(E) inclusive fitness

102. Down syndrome is commonly connected with

(A) poor prenatal care
(B) a relatively older male parent
(C) abnormal frontal lobes
(D) an iodine deficiency
(E) an abnormal 21st chromosome

103. The idea that people will alter their actions or beliefs so that their actions and beliefs are in agreement with one another is the theory of

(A) risky shift
(B) cognitive dissonance
(C) Purkinje shift
(D) self-serving bias
(E) acceptance

104. Which of the following figures built upon Weber's Law?

(A) Helmholtz
(B) Fechner
(C) Koffka
(D) Stevens
(E) Wertheimer

105. Which of the following argued that Kohlberg's moral stages were not directly applicable to females?

(A) Carol Gilligan
(B) Diana Baumrind
(C) Matina Horner
(D) Eleanor Maccoby
(E) Jenny Field

106. Which of the following personality types is NOT associated with Alfred Adler's theory of personality?

(A) sanguine
(B) choleric
(C) melancholic
(D) ectomorphic
(E) phlegmatic

107. A woman attempts to sell a car for $10,000 and then settles for $8,000. Because the seller only hoped to collect $8,000 in the first place, she was employing which of the following tactics in social psychology?

(A) reactance
(B) foot-in-the-door
(C) door-in-the-face
(D) guilt bias
(E) false cooperation

108. Which of the following is the path of a received "message" through a single neuron?

(A) presynaptic cell, cell body, axon, postsynaptic cell
(B) postsynaptic cell, cell body, axon, terminal buttons
(C) presynaptic cell, cell body, axon, dendrites
(D) dendrites, axon, cell body, terminal buttons
(E) dendrites, axon, axon hillock, terminal buttons

GO ON TO THE NEXT PAGE.

Questions 109 and 110 refer to the following study:

A researcher is studying the effect of diet on depression. The hypothesis is that a diet high in carbohydrates will help to alleviate the symptoms of depression. The sample being studied is a random sample of depressed inpatients. Every other day the subjects fill out a depression symptom inventory.

109. In the above study, the symptom inventory provides information about the

    (A) interaction effect
    (B) confounding variable
    (C) independent variable
    (D) dependent variable
    (E) control variable

110. Which of the following is the most serious confounding variable?

    (A) Some subjects are male and others are female.
    (B) Some subjects are teenagers and other subjects are in their twenties.
    (C) Some subjects have been in the hospital longer than others.
    (D) Some subjects are on anti-depressants and others are not.
    (E) Some subjects have been depressed before and others have not.

111. Which of the following is NOT a dissociative disorder?

    (A) amnesia
    (B) schizophrenia
    (C) identity disorder
    (D) fugue
    (E) multiple personality disorder

112. Behavior therapy would be most useful in treating

    (A) a childhood disorder
    (B) paranoid schizophrenia
    (C) depression
    (D) Tardive dyskenesia
    (E) a conversion disorder

113. According to Piaget, a child who looks under a pillow for a lost toy is able to appreciate

    (A) conservation
    (B) concrete operations
    (C) object permanence
    (D) exploration needs
    (E) determination

114. A subject is presented with two tones of differing intensities. The subject, however, states that the tones seem to be of the same intensity. According to Weber, this is probably because

(A) the tones were not separated by at least one just noticeable difference
(B) the tones were presented too closely together
(C) the tones were of varying pitches
(D) the subject was not motivated to pay attention
(E) response bias affected the subject

115. Hermann von Helmholtz is, in part, famous for his theory of

(A) color blindness
(B) color vision
(C) lateral inhibition
(D) sensory transduction
(E) tone deafness

116. The structuralist school of psychology viewed consciousness as

(A) divided into three separate layers
(B) a flow of ideas without clear boundaries
(C) a collective unit passed down genetically
(D) a set of discrete sensations
(E) a blank slate waiting for experience

117. The Whorfian hypothesis posits that

(A) two closely related species will develop different breeding seasons
(B) a diagnostic label influences how others interpret an individual's behavior
(C) the way an eyewitness is questioned may affect his memory of events
(D) excessive dopamine activity is a factor in schizophrenia
(E) a culture's language structure influences how the speakers perceive reality

118. According to Freud, the Oedipus complex in boys and the Electra complex in girls are resolved through

(A) moving into the latency stage
(B) identification with the opposite-sex parent
(C) identification with the same-sex parent
(D) the emergence of death instinct
(E) the strengthening of the ego

119. Which of the following figures questioned the effectiveness of psychotherapy?

(A) Abraham Maslow
(B) Hans Eysenck
(C) Melanie Klein
(D) Carol Gilligan
(E) Harry Stack Sullivan

GO ON TO THE NEXT PAGE.

120. When reciting the alphabet, children often recall A,B,C,D and X,Y,Z more readily than the letters in between. This is the result of

(A) retroactive inhibition
(B) retroactive interference
(C) proactive interference
(D) primary and secondary rehearsal
(E) primacy and recency effects

121. The concept of the reflex arc is associated with

(A) B.F. Skinner
(B) John Dewey
(C) John Watson
(D) Edward Titchener
(E) Charles Darwin

122. According to Schachter and Singer, an emotional response would involve which of the following factors in order of appearance?

(A) physiological reaction, cognition, emotion
(B) cognition, physiological reaction, emotion
(C) physiological reaction, emotion, cognition
(D) emotion, physiological reaction, cognition
(E) cognition, emotion, physiological reaction

123. Which classic experiment indicated that behavioral traits could be at least partly determined by heredity?

(A) Tyron's experiment with maze-bright and maze-dull rats
(B) Garcia's experiment with food aversion
(C) Thorndike's experiment with cats in puzzle boxes
(D) Von Frisch's experiment with honey-bees
(E) Tinbergen's experiment with stickle-back fish

124. As opposed to longitudinal design, a cross-sectional study is able to control for

(A) cohort effects
(B) demand characteristics
(C) experimenter bias
(D) the Hawthorne effect
(E) reactance

125. Proprioception is the ability to

(A) localize sound
(B) use peripheral vision
(C) sense body position
(D) sense the "nearness" of objects
(E) turn toward a stimulating cue

126. Which of the following tests includes items that discriminate between groups but that seem lacking in face validity?

   (A) Thematic Apperception Test (TAT)
   (B) Minnesota Multiphasic Personality Inventory (MMPI)
   (C) California Personality Inventory (CPI)
   (D) Q-sort
   (E) Rotter's Incomplete Sentence Blank

127. The Minnesota Multiphasic Personality Inventory (MMPI) has a validity scale which

   (A) checks for lying
   (B) increases the internal validity
   (C) increases the test-retest reliability
   (D) identifies clinically disturbed subjects
   (E) decreases scoring errors

128. Wearing uniforms has been found to promote

   (A) depressive affect
   (B) authoritarianism
   (C) deindividuation
   (D) objective self-awareness
   (E) mental creativity

129. Word order in a sentence is determined by which of the following types of rules?

   (A) phonological
   (B) morphological
   (C) prosody
   (D) syntax
   (E) semantic

130. A binocular cue used in depth perception is

   (A) good continuation
   (B) interposition
   (C) motion parallax
   (D) disparity
   (E) linear perspective

131. Which of the following groups of theorists offer stage models of development?

   (A) Piaget, Freud, and Erikson
   (B) Piaget, Freud, and Kohlberg
   (C) Freud, Maslow, and Watson
   (D) Freud, Erikson, and Kohlberg
   (E) Freud, Adler, and Piaget

GO ON TO THE NEXT PAGE.

132. Which of the following areas in the brain is the "master" of the endocrine system?

    (A) thyroid
    (B) amygdala
    (C) limbic system
    (D) thalamus
    (E) pituitary gland

133. The Acme Scale of Aggression has a +0.10 correlation with four other standardized aggression scales. Also, a correlation of +1.00 exists between the scores of any student who takes the Acme Scale of Aggression twice. This indicates that the Acme Scale of Aggression has

    (A) low internal validity but high external validity
    (B) low concurrent validity but high reliability
    (C) low face validity but high reliability
    (D) moderate external validity and moderate reliability
    (E) high content validity but low reliability

134. According to Ebbinghaus' forgetting curve, which pattern of forgetting is likely to take place after learning new material?

    (A) forgetting happens gradually and consistently
    (B) forgetting happens gradually for 24 hours and then more rapidly
    (C) forgetting happens quickly and is then offset by spontaneous recovery
    (D) forgetting happens rapidly at first and then gradually
    (E) forgetting happens in an all-or-none fashion

135. Which of the following pairs of items is incorrectly associated?

    (A) Dewey: Functionalism
    (B) Frankl: Cognitive Psychology
    (C) Adler: Individual Psychology
    (D) Titchener: Structuralism
    (E) James: Stream of Consciousness

136. Research has proven that fondling and interacting with infants enhances

    (A) motor development
    (B) physical development
    (C) emotional development
    (D) intellectual development
    (E) all of the above

137. Which of the following children would probably acquire language the slowest?

    (A) a girl exposed to only one language
    (B) a boy exposed to only one language
    (C) a girl exposed to two languages
    (D) a boy exposed to two languages
    (E) because of the LAD, all children acquire language at precisely the same rate

138. According to Piaget's cognitive stages, an individual who has just learned that water poured from a tube into a bowl maintains the same volume must have recently entered which of the following stages?

(A) accommodational
(B) sensorimotor
(C) preoperational
(D) concrete operational
(E) formal operational

139. Andrea does not like to go to parties because she knows how people will conduct themselves. She has likely developed which of the following about parties?

(A) a script
(B) a deduction
(C) a prototype
(D) a heuristic
(E) a convergence

140. Which of the following is a result of diffusion of responsibility?

(A) cooperation in a group task
(B) two-person theory of psychotherapy
(C) shyness of individuals in a large group
(D) blaming the group for individual failures
(E) tendency for individuals in a large group not to help others

141. In an attempt to separate the effects of heredity and learning, an experimenter takes a litter of cats and places each one with a different parent for rearing. This way, because the litter inherited very similar genes, the observed differences between the cats could more easily be attributed to experience. This experimental technique is called

(A) hybrid design
(B) cross fostering
(C) surrogate parenting
(D) intentional design
(E) selective breeding

142. Martin Seligman maintains that cognitive training can offset

(A) low self-esteem
(B) cognitive bias
(C) self-handicapping
(D) internal locus of control
(E) learned helplessness

143. Which of the following sensory systems involve the ganglion cells and the ciliary muscles?

(A) cutaneous
(B) auditory
(C) visual
(D) olfactory
(E) gustatory

GO ON TO THE NEXT PAGE.

144. Which of the following individuals pioneered object-relations theory?

(A) Melanie Klein
(B) Carol Gilligan
(C) Andrea Raring
(D) Mary Ainsworth
(E) Karen Horney

145. Which of the following factors has the greatest influence on interpersonal attraction?

(A) similarity of needs
(B) similarity of background
(C) polarity
(D) proximity
(E) emotional balance

146. According to Smith, Shoben, and Rip, individuals decide on the relationship between words by assessing the

(A) personal experience they have with the words
(B) acoustic similarity of the words
(C) words' respective locations in semantic hierarchies
(D) common characteristics between the words
(E) part of speech of the words

147. The idea that over-benefited people tend to feel guilty is explained through

(A) equity theory
(B) social exchange theory
(C) gain-loss theory
(D) reciprocal interaction
(E) diffusion of responsibility

148. Each of the following figures performed famous experiments in the area of conformity EXCEPT

(A) Stanley Milgram
(B) Philip Zimbardo
(C) Leon Festinger
(D) Solomon Asch
(E) Muzafer Sherif

149. A double blind experimental design is used to minimize

(A) cohort effects
(B) experimenter bias
(C) the halo effect
(D) reactance
(E) the Hawthorne effect

150. Drugs that attempt to impact behavior generally try to

(A) hinder or facilitate the transmission of "messages" at the synaptic junction
(B) speed up the action potential
(C) increase the number of neurons present in the brain
(D) stimulate the axon hillock
(E) stimulate the nodes of Ranvier

151. An individual with Wernicke's aphasia would have difficulty

(A) understanding what is said to him
(B) uttering words
(C) creating a logical sentence
(D) spelling
(E) remembering recent events

152. Learned helplessness is associated with

(A) neuroticism
(B) introversion
(C) androgyny
(D) extreme femininity scores
(E) an external locus of control

153. Each of the following factors facilitates accurate recall of a list of words from short-term memory EXCEPT

(A) acoustic similarity among the items
(B) meaningful items
(C) concrete items
(D) lack of similarity between items
(E) subject's investment in the task

154. Mr. C is passed over for a promotion at work for the fifth year. Instead of showing his anger and frustration, Mr. C responds by being the first to congratulate the promoted worker. This gracious behavior would most likely be interpreted by a psychoanalyst as

(A) repression
(B) undoing
(C) reaction formation
(D) sublimation
(E) denial

155. Which of the following individuals is associated with the discovery of secure versus insecure infant attachment?

(A) Matina Horner
(B) Anna Freud
(C) Karen Horney
(D) Diana Baumrind
(E) Mary Ainsworth

156. Which of the following is a negative symptom of schizophrenia?

(A) delusions
(B) flat affect
(C) hallucinations
(D) neologisms
(E) disorganized behavior

GO ON TO THE NEXT PAGE.

Questions 157 and 158 each refer to the following sentence:

Two bears and a donkey lived happily ever after.

157. Which of the following is true of the sentence above?
    (A) "Two cats and a dog lived happily ever after" shares the same deep structure.
    (B) The word "bears" is made up of two morphemes.
    (C) Only the word "lived" has any semantic meaning.
    (D) The sentence is structured by phonological rules.
    (E) Syntax is not employed in this sentence.

158. According to Chomsky's work, this sentence has its own, unique
    (A) surface structure
    (B) deep structure
    (C) semantic differential
    (D) morphemes
    (E) phonemes

159. Bartlett found that memory is largely
    (A) procedural
    (B) episodic
    (C) declarative
    (D) reconstructive
    (E) sensory

160. Which of the following figures is known for developing field theory?
    (A) Festinger
    (B) Asch
    (C) Heider
    (D) Triplett
    (E) Lewin

161. Absolute threshold refers to
    (A) the maximum amount of a stimulus that can be perceived
    (B) the highest intensity that can be perceived
    (C) the agreed-upon limits of a particular sensory system
    (D) the line between perception and pain in sensory systems
    (E) the minimum amount of a stimuli that can be detected 50% of the time

162. Which of the following brain areas would most likely be used for complex problem-solving?

(A) occipital lobe
(B) frontal lobe
(C) cerebellum
(D) hypothalamus
(E) hippocampus

163. Group polarization is the tendency

(A) for a group to identify a common enemy
(B) for a group to break into two opposing sides
(C) for a group to feel strongly about the dominant viewpoint
(D) for an ingroup to identify an outgroup
(E) for a group to become deadlocked during decision making

164. A researcher has performed an experiment with a random sample. He wants to test his results for statistical significance and then draw conclusions about his population. He should use which of the following type of statistics?

(A) correlations
(B) frequency distributions
(C) descriptive statistics
(D) inferential statistics
(E) referential statistics

165. Edward Tolman's theory of motivation postulated that

(A) Performance = Expectancy × Value
(B) Motivation = Need − Fear
(C) Success = Practice × Drive
(D) Performance = Drive × Habit
(E) Performance = Ability × Practice

166. Billy is a two year old. He is most likely bothered by

(A) an Oedipus complex
(B) separation anxiety and stranger anxiety
(C) castration anxiety
(D) separation anxiety and trust anxiety
(E) expression anxiety and mobility anxiety

167. Which of the following is necessary for audition?

(A) papillae
(B) amacrine cells
(C) pinna
(D) organ of corti
(E) ciliary muscles

GO ON TO THE NEXT PAGE.

168. According to Matina Horner, a woman might choose not to work because of

(A) fear of success
(B) fear of failure
(C) insecurity that success is dependent on luck
(D) self-handicapping
(E) low self-esteem

169. Which of the following is true of schizophrenia?

(A) It is more common in the upper class.
(B) It has been proven to be entirely biological.
(C) An individual with a strong social history will likely not recover.
(D) There is a lower recovery rate for process than for reactive schizophrenia.
(E) There is a lower recovery rate for reactive than for process schizophrenia.

170. According to Piaget, most five-year-old children should be in which of the following cognitive stages?

(A) accommodational
(B) sensorimotor
(C) preoperational
(D) concrete operational
(E) formal operational

171. Which of the following is referred to as white matter in the brain and spine?

(A) nerve fibers made of axons
(B) nerve fibers made of cell bodies
(C) gyri
(D) sulci
(E) bone matter

172. A random sample of students in a lecture hall could be obtained by selecting

(A) the students who raise their hands first
(B) the students with blonde hair
(C) the students with credit card numbers ending in 5
(D) every seventh student who volunteers
(E) every fifth student seated throughout the room

173. In general, people attach concepts and attributes to items and events. This knowledge is used to categorize and understand new stimuli and is best known as a person's

(A) algorithm
(B) heuristic
(C) schema
(D) mental set
(E) metacognition

174. A sign stimulus serves to trigger

 (A) a homing mechanism
 (B) a variable-interval ratio
 (C) a simple reflex
 (D) a fixed action pattern
 (E) a pheromone reaction

175. Which of the following exemplifies the illusion of control?

 (A) a teacher who believes she influences her students
 (B) a woman who practices superstitious behavior
 (C) a boy who practices positive imagery to help calm his stage fright
 (D) a girl who ties a string around her finger to remember to do something
 (E) a parent who believes that punishment is a deterrent

176. Which of the following statements about sensation is false?

 (A) Meissner's corpuscles detect temperature changes.
 (B) The organ of corti is the technical name for the ear.
 (C) Papillae are taste buds.
 (D) The tympanic membrane is the eardrum.
 (E) The olfactory bulb is located at the base of the brain.

177. Which of the following most effectively lessens group conflict?

 (A) high individual scores on the f-scale
 (B) groupthink
 (C) a charismatic leader
 (D) a superordinate goal
 (E) similarity of individuals in the group

178. In a series of learning experiments with monkeys, Harlow asserted that monkeys gained a sort of cumulative knowledge about solving problems. He came to this conclusion because with every novel problem it took the monkeys less time to learn how to solve it. Harlow called this

 (A) higher-order conditioning
 (B) simultaneous conditioning
 (C) learning to learn
 (D) trained anticipation
 (E) instinct-learning interaction

179. A city has different-sounding sirens for police, fire, and hospital vehicles. In addition, each of these vehicles can emit varying patterns of the sirens. Regardless of the type of siren heard by a line of traffic, however, the cars all know to pull to the right and clear the way. This is an example of

 (A) stimulus-response theory
 (B) stimulus discrimination
 (C) stimulus generalization
 (D) forward conditioning
 (E) operant conditioning

GO ON TO THE NEXT PAGE.

180. Which of the following concepts is NOT central to psychoanalytic theory?

(A) aggression
(B) libido
(C) free association
(D) transference
(E) animus

181. In humans, egg and sperm unite in what part of the female body?

(A) womb
(B) vagina
(C) uterus
(D) ovary
(E) fallopian tube

182. The vestibular sacs in the inner ear are essential for

(A) sensory transduction in audition
(B) detecting low frequencies
(C) detecting high frequencies
(D) physical balance
(E) proprioception

183. Robin made a grocery list of items in no particular order. She later lost the list and attempted to retrieve it from memory. When recalling items, she successfully remembered, then all of the frozen foods, and then all of the snack foods. This is an example of

(A) clustering
(B) chunking
(C) mnemonics
(D) imagery
(E) mediation

184. According to Vgotsky, what happens to the meaning that a child initially gives to a word?

(A) It creates a bias about how that child will later perceive reality.
(B) It undergoes change as the child gains experience.
(C) It consistently mirrors that of the parents.
(D) It facilitates the memorization of language.
(E) It remains stable throughout life.

185. The Bayley Scales of Infant Development do which of the following?

(A) help to identify mentally retarded infants
(B) measure intelligence in preschoolers
(C) measure IQ in preschoolers
(D) guide parents in school placement
(E) measure cognition in infants

186. Which of the following is an impulse-control disorder that involves pulling out one's own hair?

(A) Pick's disease
(B) dysthymia
(C) trichotillomania
(D) conversion disorder
(E) follicle phobia

187. Maccoby and Jacklin found that one of the few true gender differences seems to be

(A) better visual ability in girls
(B) better spatial ability in boys
(C) more compassion in girls
(D) better science skills in boys
(E) better mathematical skills in boys

188. The limbic system is crucial in the regulation of

(A) autonomic nervous system
(B) somatic nervous system
(C) hormone activity
(D) heart and lungs
(E) emotion

189. Rochel Gelman criticized Piaget's cognitive stages for

(A) ending at adolescence
(B) using unnatural testing instruments
(C) creating gender-biased stages
(D) underestimating preschoolers' ability
(E) overestimating adolescents' ability

190. According to feature detection theory, a subject would most quickly find the letter "C" if it were placed

(A) somewhere on a page amongst rows of "O"s and "Q"s
(B) somewhere on a page amongst rows of "T"s and "M"s
(C) near the top of a page amongst rows of "Q"s
(D) near the center of a page amongst rows of "O"s
(E) near the bottom of a page amongst rows of "O"s

191. Which of the following figures introduced the logic theorist, the first computer model of human problem solving?

(A) Collins and Quillian
(B) Newell and Simon
(C) Collins and Loftus
(D) Pearson
(E) Einstein

GO ON TO THE NEXT PAGE.

192. Which of the following tests allows unconscious motivation, particularly the need for achievement, to be expressed?

   (A) Minnesota Multiphasic Personality Inventory (MMPI)
   (B) Goodenough Draw-A-Person Test
   (C) Thematic Apperception Test (TAT)
   (D) California Personality Inventory (CPI)
   (E) Q-sort

193. Milgram used which theory to explain urbanites' tendency to be less social than country dwellers?

   (A) social loafing
   (B) inoculation
   (C) social facilitation
   (D) stimulus-overload
   (E) self-monitoring

194. Abraham Maslow is well known as

   (A) a forerunner of the humanistic movement in psychology
   (B) the creator of cognitive-behavioral therapy
   (C) the creator of client-centered therapy
   (D) a forerunner of object-relations theory
   (E) the creator of the archetype concept

195. Which of the following is NOT one of the personality "Big Five"?

   (A) neuroticism
   (B) agreeableness
   (C) extraversion
   (D) conscientiousness
   (E) compassion

196. Diana Baumrind found that which parenting style produces the most well-adjusted children?

   (A) authoritative
   (B) authoritarian
   (C) permissive
   (D) attached
   (E) all parenting styles were equally effective

197. Which of the following sensory system components is said to "accommodate"?

   (A) cornea
   (B) lens
   (C) retina
   (D) tympanic membrane
   (E) basilar membrane

198. Activity in which of the following areas is analyzed by lie detector tests?

   (A) central nervous system
   (B) somatic nervous system
   (C) sympathetic nervous system
   (D) parasympathetic nervous system
   (E) EEG patterns

199. Subjects in a psychology experiment attempt to remember the social security number of the person sitting next. Half of the subjects are told to put their heads down on their desks for 3 minutes. The other half of subjects are told to solve math problems for 3 minutes. If the group that solved math problems recalled the numbers as accurately as the other group did, this would support which theory of forgetting?

(A) Interference theory
(B) Trace theory
(C) Proactive inhibition theory
(D) Proactive interference theory
(E) Association theory

200. Harlow, in experiments with social isolation in monkeys, found each of the following EXCEPT that

(A) socially isolated adult females did not exhibit normal maternal behavior
(B) socially isolated adult males did not exhibit normal sexual behavior
(C) exposure to a peer group is an important factor in developing mature behavior
(D) being reared with other young monkeys provides positive socialization
(E) for normal development, monkeys must be exposed to their biological parents

201. Five hundred undergraduates were asked to report their favorite television show from a list of 100 different shows. What kind of scale can best organize the data?

(A) ordinal
(B) interval
(C) f-scale
(D) ratio
(E) nominal

202. If during a chess game a player were to write down all of the possible moves she could make, this set of moves would be an example of

(A) functional fixedness
(B) a heuristic
(C) a mental set
(D) a problem space
(E) inductive reasoning

Questions 203 and 204 refer to the following:

A speaker is attempting to convince an audience of listeners that a particular theory of evolution is correct. The audience consists of 500 adult men and women.

203. Which of the following factors would NOT increase the likelihood that the speaker will convince the audience?

(A) The speaker confidently tells the audience it will be convinced.
(B) The speaker engages in a debate with an opponent.
(C) The speaker is similar to the audience.
(D) The speaker is perceived as an expert.
(E) The speaker uses anecdotal information.

204. According to the sleeper effect, which of the following would be true?

(A) Individuals in the audience who do not pay close attention will be convinced.
(B) The message of a speaker with low credibility might be believed later.
(C) Individuals who cannot make up their minds will follow the majority opinion.
(D) Individuals who previously had no opinion on the topic will be convinced.
(E) The message will seem less convincing with the passage of time.

GO ON TO THE NEXT PAGE.

205. A rat is conditioned to press a lever to receive food. In the beginning, the rat is rewarded with food every time it presses the lever. Then, the experimenter stops rewarding the rat for this behavior and eventually the rat stops pressing the bar altogether. Three days later the rat tries pressing the bar again. This is an example of

(A) incidental learning
(B) latent responding
(C) positive transfer
(D) spontaneous recovery
(E) systematic desensitization

206. Konrad Lorenz is associated with each of the following EXCEPT

(A) the founding of ethology
(B) the study of altruism in animals
(C) research on imprinting
(D) writings on intraspecies aggression
(E) the concept of releasing stimuli

207. An individual is likely to display the most stereotypical sex-typed behavior during which of the following periods?

(A) adolescence
(B) young adulthood
(C) middle adulthood
(D) old age
(E) middle childhood

208. Which of the following is associated with Jung's analytical therapy?

(A) dream analysis
(B) transference
(C) focus on libido
(D) hypnosis
(E) defense mechanisms

209. Which of the following figures pioneered the concept of the inferiority complex?

(A) Harry Stack Sullivan
(B) Carl Rogers
(C) Abraham Maslow
(D) Alfred Adler
(E) Hans Eysenck

210. A study requires that a group of college undergraduates be present for a problem-solving workshop every other Saturday. Eventually, a number of students who want to attend fall football games drop out of the study. This is an example of

(A) cohort effects
(B) social desirability bias
(C) selective attrition
(D) nonrandom sampling
(E) reactance

211. A married couple disagrees about why the husband rarely cleans up the house. He says that he forgets. She says that he intentionally leaves the work for her. Their disagreement over the cause of his behavior is an example of:

(A) false consensus bias
(B) base-rate fallacy
(C) reciprocal interaction
(D) fundamental attribution error
(E) actor-observer attributional divergence

212. After a serious head injury, Vicky could not remember the events that led up to the accident. Vicky is likely suffering from

(A) fugue
(B) denial
(C) depression
(D) anterograde amnesia
(E) retrograde amnesia

213. Which statement explains the current view of color vision theory?

(A) Opponent process theory is thought to be superior to tri-color theory.
(B) Tri-color theory is thought to be superior to opponent-process theory.
(C) Neither opponent-process nor tri-color theories are thought to be plausible.
(D) Opponent process theory applies to retinal activity whereas tri-color theory applies to lateral geniculate activity.
(E) Opponent process theory applies to lateral geniculate activity whereas tri-color theory applies to retinal activity.

214. In his revised psychoanalytic theory, Freud named which of the following as the central source of conflict?

(A) libido
(B) superego
(C) secondary process
(D) Eros and Thanatos
(E) Pleasure Principle

215. Which of the following personality characteristics has been most closely linked to heart disease?

(A) Internal locus of control
(B) Authoritarianism
(C) Competitiveness
(D) Introversion
(E) Neuroticism

END OF TEST

ANSWER KEY

To help you zero in on any trouble areas you may have, we have provided the chapter name in which each answer below can be found. For any answers you missed, be sure to go back and review those sections carefully.

1.	A	Abnormal	46.	C	Perception	91.	E	Physiological
2.	B	Personality	47.	B	Developmental	92.	C	Learning
3.	D	Applied	48.	C	Physiological	93.	A	Ethology
4.	D	Learning	49.	C	Abnormal	94.	C	Developmental
5.	C	Developmental	50.	D	Social	95.	D	Social
6.	E	Clinical	51.	A	Learning	96.	A	Learning
7.	B	Statistics	52.	C	History	97.	B	Developmental
8.	C	Social	53.	B	Learning	98.	D	Cognition
9.	C	Ethology	54.	C	Language	99.	A	Sensation
10.	D	Language	55.	A	Developmental	100.	C	Memory
11.	A	Personality	56.	E	Perception	101.	E	Ethology
12.	E	Developmental	57.	E	Abnormal	102.	E	Abnormal
13.	A	Cognition	58.	D	Sensation	103.	B	Social
14.	E	Measurement	59.	D	Comparative	104.	B	Perception
15.	B	Abnormal	60.	B	Clinical	105.	A	Developmental
16.	A	Developmental	61.	D	Developmental	106.	D	Personality
17.	C	Memory	62.	C	Cognition	107.	C	Social
18.	D	Physiological	63.	A	Social	108.	B	Physiological
19.	A	Applied	64.	E	Personality	109.	D	Research Design
20.	E	Statistics	65.	C	Clinical	110.	D	Research Design
21.	C	Statistics	66.	B	Memory	111.	B	Abnormal
22.	B	Personality	67.	C	Developmental	112.	A	Clinical
23.	E	Social	68.	D	Physiological	113.	C	Developmental
24.	A	Social	69.	C	Abnormal	114.	A	Perception
25.	A	Language	70.	B	Social	115.	A	Sensation
26.	B	Learning	71.	B	Social	116.	D	History
27.	A	Perception	72.	A	Personality	117.	E	Language
28.	E	Cognition	73.	C	Applied	118.	C	Developmental
29.	D	Developmental	74.	E	History	119.	B	Clinical
30.	C	Abnormal	75.	D	Perception	120.	E	Memory
31.	E	History	76.	E	Learning	121.	B	History
32.	A	Memory	77.	E	Learning	122.	A	Cognition
33.	C	Social	78.	A	Statistics	123.	A	Comparative
34.	B	Language	79.	D	Personality	124.	A	Research Design
35.	D	Physiological	80.	E	Sensation	125.	C	Sensation
36.	D	Measurement	81.	D	Developmental	126.	B	Measurement
37.	B	Developmental	82.	E	Perception	127.	A	Measurement
38.	C	Personality	83.	A	Abnormal	128.	C	Social
39.	A	Social	84.	C	Measurement	129.	D	Language
40.	E	Cognition	85.	E	Social	130.	D	Perception
41.	C	Learning	86.	B	Cognition	131.	A	Developmental
42.	B	Sensation	87.	D	Abnormal	132.	E	Physiological
43.	E	Memory	88.	C	Personality	133.	B	Statistics
44.	D	Personality	89.	E	Developmental	134.	D	Memory
45.	B	Perception	90.	C	Clinical	135.	B	History

136.	E	Developmental	163.	C	Social	190.	B	Perception
137.	D	Language	164.	D	Statistics	191.	B	Cognition
138.	D	Developmental	165.	A	History	192.	C	Measurement
139.	A	Cognition	166.	B	Developmental	193.	D	Social
140.	E	Social	167.	D	Sensation	194.	A	Clinical
141.	B	Comparative	168.	A	Personality	195.	E	Personality
142.	E	Personality	169.	D	Abnormal	196.	A	Developmental
143.	C	Sensation	170.	C	Developmental	197.	B	Sensation
144.	A	Clinical	171.	A	Physiological	198.	C	Physiological
145.	D	Social	172.	E	Research Design	199.	B	Memory
146.	D	Cognition	173.	C	Cognition	200.	E	Comparative
147.	A	Social	174.	D	Ethology	201.	E	Statistics
148.	C	Social	175.	B	Social	202.	D	Cognition
149.	B	Research Design	176.	A	Sensation	203.	A	Social
150.	A	Physiological	177.	D	Social	204.	B	Social
151.	C	Language	178.	C	Comparative	205.	D	Learning
152.	E	Personality	179.	C	Learning	206.	B	Ethology
153.	A	Memory	180.	E	Clinical	207.	B	Developmental
154.	C	Clinical	181.	E	Developmental	208.	A	Clinical
155.	E	Developmental	182.	D	Sensation	209.	D	Clinical
156.	B	Abnormal	183.	A	Memory	210.	C	Research Design
157.	B	Language	184.	B	Language	211.	E	Social
158.	A	Language	185.	A	Measurement	212.	E	Abnormal
159.	D	Memory	186.	C	Abnormal	213.	E	Sensation
160.	E	Social	187.	B	Personality	214.	D	Clinical
161.	E	Perception	188.	E	Physiological	215.	C	Personality
162.	B	Physiological	189.	D	Developmental			

PART **IV**

Appendix: The Admissions Process

23

Going Back
To School

MAKING SENSE OF DEGREE DISTINCTIONS

If you're thinking of becoming a psychologist, you should know that there are many permutations of the old Freudian stereotype. Graduate schools offer different models, different degrees, and different areas of concentration. Understanding the different degree options prior to the application process is crucial. Basically, you must make three decisions:

- What kind of psychologist do you want to be?

  This will isolate the training model right for you.

- What degree is right for your career goals?

  This will determine the specific degree you pursue.

- What area of concentration interests you?

  This will help you prioritize one school over another.

Each of these decisions, in turn, will narrow the list of schools that are appropriate for you. Ultimately, you will be left with those that have programs matching your career and training goals. Applying to schools that do not match your career goals is a waste of time and money. The admissions committees will see that you are not a good match for their programs and toss you out immediately.

So, let's make some decisions . . .

DECISION 1: WHAT KIND OF PSYCHOLOGIST DO YOU WANT TO BE?

The American Psychological Association (APA) recognizes three distinct types of psychologists: the research scientist, the scientist-practitioner, and the professional psychologist. Some overlap exists among the types, but there are significant differences in training and career paths. Graduate program descriptions clearly state what type of psychologist their programs train and, therefore, what training model they follow. Apply only to schools that train the type you'd like to be.

Research scientist

Pro: Incredible research training. Perfect for academic types.

Con: All the research.

The original type of psychologist was the research scientist. Back in the day of Wilhelm Wundt and William Sheldon, the field of psychology emerged as the scientific study of the mind and behavior. Its goal was to further knowledge about the science of the mind. As psychology is a relatively young science, many psychologists today are employed for this sole purpose: to further the field. Most of your university professors are research scientists. Even more research scientists are employed by businesses and the government.

The primary activity for a research scientist is . . . research. Research psychologists conduct, supervise, and write about research. Research, research, research! If that is your interest, research psychology is for you. If you do not have a passion for research, then stay away from graduate programs that produce research scientists.

Many psychology departments in high-ranking public and private universities train only research scholars. No counseling or clinical training will be provided in such a training model, so if your goal is to work with people as a counselor, then this type of school is not for you.

Scientist-practitioner

Pro: **The degree you can take anywhere.**

Con: **The incredible competition for admission.**

The scientist-practitioner training model emerged from a psychology conference held in Boulder, Colorado, in 1949. Thus, this model is often referred to as the Boulder model. The Boulder model was born out of a need to train psychologists in practical as well as research skills as more people sought out treatment through psychology. The goal of the scientist-practitioner training model is to develop psychologists who can both conduct research and practice in the areas of applied psychology.

Although it may sound as if this is a degree for the "people-person" psychologist, don't forget about the "scientist" part in the scientist-practitioner model. The model was developed in order to balance practice and research, but scientist-practitioner programs overwhelmingly emphasize research. Basically, scientist-practitioners are research scientists who are also trained to assess and treat patients. However, most of their assessment and treatment is ultimately related to research in the works.

The scientist-practitioner training model is most commonly used to train students who specialize in the area of clinical psychology. Clinical psychologists generally go on to work in clinical settings, such as hospitals, where they also conduct research, or they settle into a university research setting where they may also practice or supervise clinical work.

Note that in order to emphazie the scientist part of the scientist-practioner model, some clinical psychology programs have re-named themselves clinical science programs.

Professional psychologist

Pro: **Focuses entirely on training practicing psychologists.**

Con: **May carry less academic prestige.**

The professional training model was first structured at a conference in Vail, Colorado. The Vail model was born out of the desire of many psychologists to be trained solely as clinical practitioners. This training model develops clinicians, not researchers. It is appropriate for anyone who wants to work primarily (if not entirely) with people in a counseling setting. Little or no research training will be provided.

The professional model (unlike the research and scientist-practitioner models, which are generally university-based) can be found in either a university setting or a freestanding professional school. This is where the problem lies. It is no secret that the professional model is perceived by many in academic settings as inferior training compared to the other two models. There are three reasons for this perception: The professional model is the newest model to emerge, it is less concerned with research and academics, and it is often housed in schools that are not necessarily held to the same standards as universities.

If you know that you want to be exclusively a working clinician, the professional model is right for you. Just be sure to do your homework and find a school that can provide a respectable degree.

DECISION 2: WHICH DEGREE IS RIGHT FOR YOUR CAREER GOALS?

If you have purchased this book, you are most likely considering a doctoral degree in psychology. (Most masters programs do not, in fact, require the GRE Psychology Test for admission and some do not require any GRE test at all.) It is important to be well informed about the different degree options because even though various degrees may all fall within the area of psychology, the roads and the destinations for these degrees are actually quite different.

M.A. The terminal master's degree

Pro: **2–3 year program, easier to get into, a sufficient degree for many career goals.**

Con: **M.A. is not a psychologist.**

The terminal master's program is a *master's only* program. This means that the training culminates with a master's degree; the option of continuing on for your doctorate does not exist. While a master's degree will not earn you the title of *psychologist* (you need a doctorate for that), it does imply expertise in the field. For many jobs, this will be all you need. Also, the master's degree programs are shorter, less costly, and easier to get into than doctorate programs.

As for the negatives, the APA recognizes only doctorates as true psychologists. In fact, psychology master's programs have been quite a debate for the APA. In many states, holders of master's degrees cannot practice independently without supervision. So your best bet is to decide what kind of job you'd like to hold, then find out what degree is required for such a job. The moral of the story: a master's degree and a doctorate are not interchangeable.

Ph.D. The doctor of philosophy

Pros: **The highest level of accomplishment. Better money and jobs than M.A.**

Cons: **The rigorous admissions obstacle. The 4–7 year program length.**

A doctor of philosophy or Ph.D. is by far the most recognized and awarded doctorate degree in psychology. The professors you had in college all probably had Ph.D.s, whether their field was art history, English, psychology, or so on. It is the old standard, and many assert that it is the most respected degree in terms of training and experience. A Ph.D. will prepare you for a career involving research, writing, teaching, or practice, depending on which school you attend and what its training model is. Ph.D. programs may use the research-scientist model, the scientist-practitioner model, or the professional model depending on the focus of the particular program.

So why doesn't everyone run out and get a Ph.D.? The cold hard facts about Ph.D. programs in psychology are this: they are incredibly hard to get into, and then you can expect to be a poor graduate student for at least 4–7 years. Psychology Ph.D. programs (especially in the clinical area) have been called the toughest graduate programs to get into today—harder than medical school or veterinary school. In fact, these days, it is actually easier to become a psychiatrist than a psychologist. Because there are so few spaces available per year in these doctorate programs, the competition is keen. The best graduate schools accept only about 2 percent of their applicants!

Psy.D. The doctor of psychology

Pros: **The practical and applied focus. Little or no boring research.**

Cons: **Possible negative perception of the degree compared to a Ph.D.**

While the title Ph.D. does not indicate any one training model, the Psy.D. degree was created specifically for professional training model programs. The concept of the Psy.D. originated from the idea that there should be a distinct degree that accompanies professional training (as opposed to research-scientist or scientist-practitioner training). The Psy.D. indicates a stronger focus and expertise in the practical and applied areas. The Ph.D. indicates a stronger scientific or academic base. Sounds simple enough, right?

The distinctions between the Ph.D. and the Psy.D. have not turned out quite so neatly. While anyone with a Psy.D. definitely has been trained with the professional model, someone with a Ph.D. may have been trained with the research-scientist, scientist-practitioner, or professional model. The reason for this is that students trained with the research-scientist model or with the scientist-practitioner model are awarded Ph.D.s; students trained in the professional model, however, may receive either a Ph.D. or a Psy.D. depending on the school. Because the Psy.D. is the newest degree mutation, some schools have shied away from using the degree title over the Ph.D.

DECISION 3: WHAT AREA OF CONCENTRATION INTERESTS YOU?

So, last but not least, once you have decided how you would like to be trained and what degree you should go for, you are left to decide what area of psychology interests you most. This is usually a fun, easy decision compared to the first two. The questions to ask yourself are: What psychology classes did I enjoy the most in college? What specific topics would I like to focus on throughout my graduate experience? What area of concentration most relates to the job I envision for myself? In what area do I want to become an expert?

Below are the major areas of concentration (although new areas are slowly emerging):

Clinical psychologists are concerned with mental illness and therapy. The majority of clinical training revolves around assessing, researching, and treating various mental illnesses. For this reason, most clinical programs use the scientist-practitioner model. The mental conditions that clinical students are trained to work with vary from the everyday difficulties to the most severe mental disorders. Most clinical students focus on particular disorders or specific clinical issues. Clinical psychologists may work in universities, hospitals, clinics, or private practice depending on their specific training or interests.

Cognitive psychologists study cognitive processes such as how people know things, think about things, and organize things in their minds. Specific topics covered in cognitive psychology are the processes of thought, knowledge, memory, and language. Most often cognitive psychologists are trained with a research-scientist model and can be found in university or laboratory settings.

Community psychologists are concerned with communities of people rather than individuals. In some ways, they are similar to sociologists in that they study groups of people and how their surroundings influence overall behavior. Community psychologists often study special populations, especially groups that might be at risk for emotional or behavioral difficulty. Community psychology seems to be most available in big city schools. Community psychologists often work with health agencies, schools, or community offices to promote optimal conditions for people.

Counseling psychologists focus more on problems that people normally encounter as part of life rather than on actual mental illnesses. Students in this area might learn to assess, treat, and research problems related to careers, relationships, death, stress, transitions, and other life span occurrences. Counseling psychologists work in university, hospital, clinical, or private settings, depending on their particular area of specialty.

Developmental psychologists specialize in normal human development over the life span. Students in this area are given a strong base in normal development patterns. Issues related to ages, stages, and changes are of particular interest to developmental psychologists. Different topics they might examine developmentally include behavior, emotion, cognition, language, and sex. Developmental psychologists serve as researchers, professors, and experts for the particular issues they know best.

Experimental psychologists are most closely compared to the "original" psychologists such as Wilhelm Wundt. They are primarily concerned with conducting experiments on people and animals in order to learn more about behavior, cognition, physiology, or emotion. Experimental psychologists are obviously best trained through a research-scientist method. Ultimately, these psychologists might conduct research and teach for universities, corporate labs, or the government.

Health psychologists are interested in the link between psychology and physical well being. They examine the interplay of what we do and how we feel. Health psychologists help us understand how we can use our minds to be healthier. This is a broad area that may include the prevention of or recovery from illness, the overall links between habit and health, or the definition of healthy psychological environments.

Industrial psychologists study people, jobs, and job settings. They look for problems and solutions in the areas of career placement, hiring, work environment, and production. Overall, the goal is to increase efficiency or success of an industry through optimal management of employees. Industrial psychologists most commonly work for universities, industries, or the government.

Physiological psychologists study the relationship between the physical and the psychological. They investigate what physical systems might cause people or other animals to behave in certain ways. They explore how our emotions and behaviors also affect our physiology. This area of psychology is strongly focused on the physical sciences and so most students are trained using a research-scientist method. Physiological psychologists may work in a range of settings depending on their specialty.

Psychometrics psychologists are the number crunchers of psychology. They are trained extensively in quantitative methods (numbers and statistics, that is). Psychometric experts design psychological tests, research methods, and research designs. While most Ph.D. students are required to develop a strong base in statistics and research methodology, students of psychometrics focus almost entirely on designing systems to acquire and scrutinize information. Psychometric psychologists most often work in university, corporate, or government settings.

Social psychologists study people in groups and individuals in relation to society. They are concerned with why people act or think in a certain way based on group or societal influences. Particular topics include attitudes, dynamics, group patterns, socialization, influence, prejudice, gender, and the like. These topics apply to behavioral and societal issues such as war, television, advertising, aggression, group behavior, and more. Because this is such broad field, a social psychologist may find work in wide range of environments.

24

Candidacy

HOW DO YOU LOOK?

Graduate psychology programs receive hundreds of applications. In the end, each school will accept only a handful from the applicant pool. The upside to the competitive craziness is the fact that schools make no bones about what you need to be a competitive candidate. The range of sources—from application information to APA literature—largely agree on the key selection criteria.

THE FIRST CUT

Because programs receive hundreds more applications than they accept, schools make it easy on themselves and begin the first cut process with the tangible, empirical figures. Some schools create some sort of math equation using your test scores and GPA; other schools have GRE or GPA cutoffs. Mostly, they begin by comparing numbers one way or another. The applicants with the highest numbers pass "GO" and proceed to the next cut.

The first cut factors are:

GPA

- Calculated from all undergraduate work
- Calculated from last two years of undergraduate work
- Calculated from psychology course work only

GRE Scores

- GRE Verbal
- GRE Quantitative
- GRE Analytical or Analytical Writing
- GRE Psychology Subject Test

How impressive you look at first glance

- Where you earned your undergraduate degree
- Your curriculum vita
- Your personal statement
- Who wrote your references

THE SECOND CUT

If you meet the first criteria, then your application will advance toward a second examination. The second cut involves other factors that might demonstrate your exceptional potential. Various program types emphasize different criteria, but there is general agreement about what these more subjective criteria are:

Being published

Nothing looks better than being published. If you are senior author, second author, or any author on a scholarly work that has been published in a respectable journal, you are head and shoulders above everyone else.

Research experience

Research experience is most heavily weighted by academic programs rather than by professional programs. Still, it seems to give you the inside track today. Without research experience, great grades and high scores are just not a complete package. Many students obtain volunteer research experience while undergraduates or after college. For the more competitive schools, research experience is a must.

Letters of recommendation

These are best written by a professor or employer who knows you very well, has outstanding things to say about you, and preferably is very well known in his/her field. Generally, two of the three letters required need to be from people in the field of psychology. If you have been out of school for a while, you might include one letter that is relevant to your recent activity. No casual references or references from your own therapist please. The more prestigious the letter writer, the better.

Statement of purpose

Your statement of purpose must be focused and specific. It should clearly demonstrate that you have done your homework. Focus on your specific plans and how each particular school and its faculty will help you meet these goals. The more direct links you are able to make between what you have done, what you want to do, and the particular school you are addressing, the better. Make every school seem like the missing piece in the grand plan of your psychology career. Though you may send similar essays to different schools, do not even think about sending the same one to all schools. Another important taboo is being too general in your essay about your plans for school and after. You need to have a specific area you want to pursue or a specific career goal. Without this, it is difficult to determine whether you are applying to the correct programs. Someone with a specific plan will get the spot.

Undergraduate honors program/thesis

You can get a lot of mileage out of an undergraduate thesis. Depending on the nature of the project, an undergraduate thesis might entail research work, statistical tests, and an APA-style final paper. If you do quality work, your thesis advisors are good candidates for recommendation letters. Also, if you believe it will be well received, you might want to enclose this undergraduate thesis with your application.

Clinical experience

Although clinical experience is not essential, it is helpful. It will generally be weighted more heavily by professional programs than by research programs. Most applicants have had some form of clinical experience through working on a hotline or at a shelter. Some applicants will have more intense clinical experience.

Awards received throughout your academic career

Every application requests that you list awards and honors earned in college. The more that you are able to list here, the better.

Undergraduate course of study/course load

For the second cut, the department examines not only your grades but also what type of course load you carried in college. The essential courses include statistics, experimental, developmental, and abnormal psychology. Also, schools like to see a broad undergraduate education that includes subjects other than psychology. The "hard science" courses are particularly impressive. Course loads that are too light or that contain too many easy classes are not impressive.

THE THIRD CUT

After the above criteria are examined and weighed, some schools choose the applicants they want from the second cut and offer them admission. Other programs, especially super-competitive or clinical programs, have an interview process. The interview process coupled with a re-examination of your application materials is the third and final stage for these schools. After all interviews are given, the department will make its final decision. Information and tips for the interview are offered in the next chapter.

25

The Application Process

WE'RE NOT IN KANSAS ANYMORE

Once you begin to work your way through the graduate school application process, you will soon realize that the process barely resembles college admissions. The application process for graduate school will require more time, more initiative, and more work than any other application process you have encountered.

More time than you probably think must be allotted to compete successfully. Thoroughly researching schools takes time. Most Ph.D. programs require GRE General *and* Subject tests. College professors need a significant amount of lead-time to complete recommendations. Personal essays will evolve through many revisions. Competition is keen, and a hasty effort will hurt your chances.

The best time to begin thinking about the application process is at least a year to nine months before the applications are actually due. Because most applications are due between December 15 and January 15, ideally, you should begin the process in the spring of that year by perhaps knocking one of the required tests out of the way. Of course, it is possible to begin the process in the fall.

More initiative on your part will increase the likelihood that you are admitted to a graduate school that is a suitable match for your goals. Though resources like this book exist to help you make sense of the task at hand, the effort must not end here. You will need a wealth of information to make wise choices concerning degree distinctions, department areas, and program emphases. Most likely, this information will come from a variety of sources.

More work for you is what all of this boils down to. It hardly seems fair to make the process so overwhelming, but look at it from the graduate schools' perspective. Most psychology departments turn away qualified applicants every year just because there are so few spaces available. If the application process weeds out those frightened of hard work, so be it.

If you're not scared away yet, then bear with us. The Princeton Review is here to make your life easier. We have already done most of the prep work for you. We have researched the field and the application process. We have created a step-by-step checklist to ensure that you leave nothing out. The Princeton Review is the yellow brick road you need.

HOW TO RESEARCH SCHOOLS

Your initial research into graduate programs in psychology need only be concerned with the basics. To begin, you must know what schools offer the specific degree that you want, the descriptive statistics for the programs that interest you, and how to contact these schools for further information.

Without a doubt, the best source for this information is the *Graduate Study in Psychology* guide published by the American Psychological Association (APA). The guide profiles every APA accredited program and every department that offers a Ph.D., Psy.D., or M.A. in the different areas of psychology. Information provided includes:

- Department addresses and contact numbers

- Accredited degrees offered

- Orientation and objectives of each department

- Number of faculty, students, and degrees awarded each year

- Degree requirements

- Admission requirements (required coursework, scores, GPA, other criteria)

- Tuition, housing, financial assistance

Clearly, the APA guide should be your initial resource. Unfortunately, the guide can be difficult to locate. Your best bet is the bookstore of a large university. You can also pay to access it online at the APA website, www.APA.org or order it directly from the APA by calling (800) 374-2721 or e-mailing order@apa.org.

BROWSING FOR SCHOOLS

Early on in your search, you should be open-minded in your school search. If you cross a school off of your list at this point, it is unlikely that you will ever revisit it as an option. On the other hand, you cannot realistically consider every school that offers a degree in your area of interest. If you are working from the APA guide, you are probably looking at 200 to 300 departments that offer the degree that you want. The question is how to make a list of potential schools that is neither too broad nor too narrow.

At this point in the game, you are browsing rather than shopping to buy. Your list should include anything you might want. Because you might be clearer on what you don't want than what you do want, start by eliminating programs that you know do not suit you. Consider these factors:

- **School Rank.** Consult a current rank order of schools. Browse through the APA guide and see what mean GPA and GRE scores are required for schools in the different tiers. Your browsing list should probably include 20–30 schools with the majority of them being in a realistic tier for you. You will also want to include in this list up to 5 reach schools (schools that you are less likely to get into) and 5 backup schools (schools that should easily accept you).

- **Location.** Though no one will advise you to choose your graduate program based on the scenery, location can be an important factor. Let's be realistic! Ph.D. programs last an average of 4–7 years, and there are certain places where you just may not be happy for that long. Don't worry so much about where you do want to live, but cross out programs that are in states or areas where you know you don't want to live.

- **School Type.** Some applicants have a preference for schools based on general characteristics, such as size, public vs. private, etc.

- **Personal Circumstances.** Of course, there are those personal circumstances that we all have to consider. If you are married, have a house and two children, and no one wants to move, you don't need to spend time researching schools on the other side of the country. Cross off schools that are not realistic options for you based on your personal situation.

SHOPPING TO BUY

You must carefully examine the schools on your browsing list in order to make wise decisions about a final list. Applicants generally do this by contacting the schools to which they might apply and request all information and application materials. Scrutinizing this material will provide more information than any other source.

The key elements of programs that deserve your attention are:

- **Theoretical Orientation.** It is important to know the "slant" of a department. Many departments align themselves with a particular theoretical orientation, such as behavioral or psychodynamic. Other departments choose to be eclectic and employ faculty of various emphases. Be sure that your interests match the general mission of the department.

- **Appropriate Mentors.** Once you have decided a general topic that you are interested in pursuing (let's say depression), find departments that house more than one faculty member with whom you might like to work. When examining department literature, look for one faculty member who is working on your general topic of interest, as well as one or two other faculty members whose work is of interest to you. Don't put all of your eggs in one faculty member's basket; often, students' interests change over time or they discover that Dr. Friendly is not so friendly after all.

- **Amount of Clinical Work and Supervision.** If your department area includes clinical training, this training generally starts the second year. Find out the ratio of hours of supervision per week to the hours of casework per week. Some departments assign larger and smaller caseloads. Look for a ratio that suits your needs.

- **Required Research.** Different schools prioritize research differently. Be honest with yourself about what kind of training you want.

- **Curriculum.** Most schools will include a sample curriculum with the information that they distribute. Compare curriculums of different schools and pinpoint the differences.

- **Training Facilities.** Department literature will also include descriptive information about department facilities and school resources. Most departments have adequate facilities. If you have a particular interest in an area that requires certain technology, identify programs that have these resources.

- **Tuition Waiver.** Some schools "remit" tuition upon acceptance. What this means is that if you are accepted, you don't have to pay for school. Generally, it is the big schools that can afford to do this for their graduate students. Students end up earning their keep through the work they do in the department.

- **Amount of Stipend.** In addition to tuition remittance, schools may offer a stipend. Students work for this money by carrying out research assistantships or teaching assistantships. These assistantships are usually a required part of the training, and they enable students to support themselves by working in the department. Stipends may range from $1,000 to $14,000 per year. Match departmental resources with your own financial needs.

- **Program Atmosphere.** An important part of any school or workplace is its atmosphere. Probably the best way to get a feel for a program is to visit, have an interview, or talk to graduate students in the department.

THE CHEAT SHEET

Though your application materials will certainly not include an etiquette book, particular standards are expected throughout the process, and you are somehow expected to know them. Consider the following tips a cheat sheet.

THE APPLICATION

- In September, call for applications or check to see if they can be downloaded or submitted via the web. September is usually when the most recent materials are available. Some schools take their sweet time in mailing out the material, and others send the applications by bulk mail, which is notoriously slow. Don't wait until November.

- Always request two applications from each department and make a photocopy of the application when the materials arrive. This will leave you with two official copies and one unofficial copy. Keep one official application from each department in a safe place; this will be your emergency backup copy.

- Weed through and organize the materials when you receive them. Make a master list of deadlines. Don't accumulate a confusing mass of paperwork.

- Don't even think about handwriting your applications. Fill out the photocopy of your application in handwritten form, as you will want it to be typed. This will be your rough draft.

- Limit your answers to the space provided whenever possible. Try to minimize the amount of searching and page flipping that the reader will have to do.

- Your final application should be completely free of typos, white out, and coffee stains. Have someone proofread your final application. It must be perfect.

- Photocopy your completed final application to keep for your records. Occasionally, applications are lost. More likely, you will want to remember what you wrote when it comes time for the interview.

- Mail your application at least one week before the deadline. Note that most deadlines refer to receipt deadlines rather than postmark deadlines. Never work too close to the closing date in case of a last minute catastrophe.

- Do not call and harass department secretaries about whether your application was received. If you are really concerned, send it by certified mail.

THE PERSONAL STATEMENT

- The personal statement is one of the most weighty factors in your application. Once the department has grouped people by number-crunching grades and scores, its first look at you as a person will come through the personal statement. Your statement must be stellar; its importance cannot be overstated!

- The questions asked in the personal statement vary from school to school. Generally, the personal essay will focus on some of the following areas: career plans, areas of interest, faculty of interest, clinical and research experience, autobiographical information, and why you have applied to a particular area or school. Absolutely do not send the same essay to every school. Answer the specific questions posed to you by each school and tailor the essay toward that school.

- Unlike college essays, there is little room for creativity in your graduate school statement. Although some creativity or emphasis on your unique strengths will help you stand apart, schools are really looking for impressive information and serious objectives. Don't be cute or immature in your style.

- Have a purpose. Don't be wishy-washy about what you want to study. Choose one or two goals you are interested in and focus on these as clear goals. Of course, these things should be aligned with the work of the department.

- Pick one or two faculty members that you want to work with and include them in your essay. Refer to work they have done or articles they have written. Most applicants will not go to such lengths. (You can find articles through a Psychology Lit search at a library or on the Internet.)

- Flirt with every school. Make every school your first choice. Tailor your application essay to fit the department. The more specific you can be about the work of department faculty or about the department itself, the better. This shows that you have done your research and that you really want to go to that particular school.

- Work, work, and more work. Your essay should evolve through at least three revisions. Have two proofreaders at each stage that can comment on content, effectiveness, and grammar.

RECOMMENDATION LETTERS

- Most departments require three recommendation letters. At least two of these three should be written by professors or professionals in the field of psychology who are familiar with your work or your potential. The third could be written by someone who can evaluate you on some unique and impressive basis. Recommendation letters should never be casual character references written by friends or therapists.

- Do not even bother obtaining letters from people who cannot recommend you strongly. Your references must know you and be able to write specific and positive accomplishments.

- Always waive your right to see the reference letter. This is the expected standard. If you are nervous about what someone might say about you, it is probably best to look elsewhere for a recommendation.

- Send the reference forms and any helpful information (transcripts, resumes, letter of intent) to your references with plenty of time to spare. Also, clearly mark deadlines and department addresses. Allow your references at least one month to complete this task. Professors do not take kindly to last minute recommendation requests.

- Always inform your references of your final decisions about school. If they recommend you, they care about where you go!

NETWORKING

- Call professors, graduate students, or professionals that you know in psychology and pick their brains for information about the field, departments, or faculty. No one knows the process better than they do.

- Write a formal letter to departmental faculty with whom you might like to work. Tell them about your interest in their work and articles. Let them know you are applying and are hoping to work with them. Do not expect a response to these letters. They simply put your name in the air. Such letters of interest should be sent in the fall, before application deadlines. Once applications are in, any attempt to contact faculty would be suspect. Also, no casual phone calls or random visits please.

THE INTERVIEW

- Prepare and practice. Prepare for your interview by reviewing materials about the department and by reviewing articles written by your chosen faculty. Practice answers to common questions. Be prepared to talk about anything that was addressed in your personal statement.

- When you visit a school, stay with graduate students if possible. This will ensure that you get a casual behind-the-scenes look at the department. Some students even help in the selection process, so it helps to get to know them. Never forget, however, that you are being watched! Keep your best foot forward at all times.

- Dress conservatively for interviews: suits for men and suits or tailored dresses for women.

- Be personable. Often, at interviews, the faculty want to see how well you relate with others or how easily they could work with you for many years. Have a personality. Show them you can handle yourself under pressure.

- Don't be shy. Let the faculty see your enthusiasm and your assertiveness. Let them know you have goals and that you want to be admitted. Lack of enthusiasm during an interview weekend could be very costly.

APPLICATION TIMETABLE AND CHECKLIST

SPRING

❏   Take either the GRE General Test or the GRE Psychology Subject Test.

SUMMER

❏   Begin to research schools.
❏   Obtain the APA *Graduate Study in Psychology* guide.
❏   Make a list of schools for browsing.

SEPTEMBER

❏   Request department information and two applications for schools on your browsing list.
❏   Photocopy the blank applications you receive.
❏   Using department information, research the schools on your browsing list even further.
❏   Call students or faculty that you know in the field for further information about programs.
❏   Get involved in local research or clinical experience.

OCTOBER

❏   Take any remaining GRE tests. Warning: The December subject test date is too late for many schools.
❏   Finalize your list. You are now shopping to buy. This list generally includes 10–20 schools.
❏   Make a master list of deadlines and required material for the schools on your final list.
❏   Line up your references.
❏   Write to one faculty member in each department on your final list.
❏   Begin the first draft of your personal essays.

NOVEMBER

❏   Have your essays critiqued for content, uniqueness, effectiveness, and grammar.
❏   Revise essays as needed.
❏   Request your college transcripts.
❏   Send recommendation information to references at least one month in advance.
❏   Call ETS or check your GRE score report to confirm that your scores have been sent.

DECEMBER

❏   Finish your applications. No typos. Keep a blank copy of each application, just in case.
❏   Revisit your master checklist for individual school deadlines.
❏   Make a photocopy of the completed applications for your records.
❏   Mail your completed applications and fees at least one week before deadline.
❏   Relax . . . it is out of your hands for now.

JANUARY, FEBRUARY, MARCH

❑   Wait to hear about interviews, if applicable.
❑   Practice and prepare for your interviews if you are offered any.
❑   Wait to hear about acceptances.
❑   Evaluate offers as quickly a possible. Don't hold on to too many.

APRIL

❑   Make your final decisions by April 15.
❑   Call or write to your references. Tell them what you decided and thank them for their help.
❑   CELEBRATE!

ABOUT THE AUTHOR

Meg Jay, M.A., is a Doctoral Candidate in Clinical Psychology at the University of California, Berkeley; she earned her master's degree from this program. She has a minor in Quantitative Psychology, in which the focus is test construction and validation. Ms. Jay taught her first Princeton Review class more than ten years ago at age 20, and she now teaches GRE, MCAT, LSAT, and GMAT courses for The Princeton Review. In addition, Ms. Jay serves as a master-trainer for new teachers, works on the development of new materials for the LSAT and MCAT, and has been recognized in national teacher competitions. Ms. Jay also instructs various psychology classes at the University of California, and she has recently served on the graduate admissions committee for the clinical program. Despite having GRE General and Subject scores in the 99th percentile and a summa cum laude B.A. in Psychology from the University of Virginia, Ms. Jay was not admitted to every graduate school to which she applied; fortunately, Berkeley was her first choice.

GRE SUBJECT TEST

#						#						#						#					
1	Ⓐ	Ⓑ	Ⓒ	Ⓓ	Ⓔ	56	Ⓐ	Ⓑ	Ⓒ	Ⓓ	Ⓔ	111	Ⓐ	Ⓑ	Ⓒ	Ⓓ	Ⓔ	166	Ⓐ	Ⓑ	Ⓒ	Ⓓ	Ⓔ
2	Ⓐ	Ⓑ	Ⓒ	Ⓓ	Ⓔ	57	Ⓐ	Ⓑ	Ⓒ	Ⓓ	Ⓔ	112	Ⓐ	Ⓑ	Ⓒ	Ⓓ	Ⓔ	167	Ⓐ	Ⓑ	Ⓒ	Ⓓ	Ⓔ
3	Ⓐ	Ⓑ	Ⓒ	Ⓓ	Ⓔ	58	Ⓐ	Ⓑ	Ⓒ	Ⓓ	Ⓔ	113	Ⓐ	Ⓑ	Ⓒ	Ⓓ	Ⓔ	168	Ⓐ	Ⓑ	Ⓒ	Ⓓ	Ⓔ
4	Ⓐ	Ⓑ	Ⓒ	Ⓓ	Ⓔ	59	Ⓐ	Ⓑ	Ⓒ	Ⓓ	Ⓔ	114	Ⓐ	Ⓑ	Ⓒ	Ⓓ	Ⓔ	169	Ⓐ	Ⓑ	Ⓒ	Ⓓ	Ⓔ
5	Ⓐ	Ⓑ	Ⓒ	Ⓓ	Ⓔ	60	Ⓐ	Ⓑ	Ⓒ	Ⓓ	Ⓔ	115	Ⓐ	Ⓑ	Ⓒ	Ⓓ	Ⓔ	170	Ⓐ	Ⓑ	Ⓒ	Ⓓ	Ⓔ
6	Ⓐ	Ⓑ	Ⓒ	Ⓓ	Ⓔ	61	Ⓐ	Ⓑ	Ⓒ	Ⓓ	Ⓔ	116	Ⓐ	Ⓑ	Ⓒ	Ⓓ	Ⓔ	171	Ⓐ	Ⓑ	Ⓒ	Ⓓ	Ⓔ
7	Ⓐ	Ⓑ	Ⓒ	Ⓓ	Ⓔ	62	Ⓐ	Ⓑ	Ⓒ	Ⓓ	Ⓔ	117	Ⓐ	Ⓑ	Ⓒ	Ⓓ	Ⓔ	172	Ⓐ	Ⓑ	Ⓒ	Ⓓ	Ⓔ
8	Ⓐ	Ⓑ	Ⓒ	Ⓓ	Ⓔ	63	Ⓐ	Ⓑ	Ⓒ	Ⓓ	Ⓔ	118	Ⓐ	Ⓑ	Ⓒ	Ⓓ	Ⓔ	173	Ⓐ	Ⓑ	Ⓒ	Ⓓ	Ⓔ
9	Ⓐ	Ⓑ	Ⓒ	Ⓓ	Ⓔ	64	Ⓐ	Ⓑ	Ⓒ	Ⓓ	Ⓔ	119	Ⓐ	Ⓑ	Ⓒ	Ⓓ	Ⓔ	174	Ⓐ	Ⓑ	Ⓒ	Ⓓ	Ⓔ
10	Ⓐ	Ⓑ	Ⓒ	Ⓓ	Ⓔ	65	Ⓐ	Ⓑ	Ⓒ	Ⓓ	Ⓔ	120	Ⓐ	Ⓑ	Ⓒ	Ⓓ	Ⓔ	175	Ⓐ	Ⓑ	Ⓒ	Ⓓ	Ⓔ
11	Ⓐ	Ⓑ	Ⓒ	Ⓓ	Ⓔ	66	Ⓐ	Ⓑ	Ⓒ	Ⓓ	Ⓔ	121	Ⓐ	Ⓑ	Ⓒ	Ⓓ	Ⓔ	176	Ⓐ	Ⓑ	Ⓒ	Ⓓ	Ⓔ
12	Ⓐ	Ⓑ	Ⓒ	Ⓓ	Ⓔ	67	Ⓐ	Ⓑ	Ⓒ	Ⓓ	Ⓔ	122	Ⓐ	Ⓑ	Ⓒ	Ⓓ	Ⓔ	177	Ⓐ	Ⓑ	Ⓒ	Ⓓ	Ⓔ
13	Ⓐ	Ⓑ	Ⓒ	Ⓓ	Ⓔ	68	Ⓐ	Ⓑ	Ⓒ	Ⓓ	Ⓔ	123	Ⓐ	Ⓑ	Ⓒ	Ⓓ	Ⓔ	178	Ⓐ	Ⓑ	Ⓒ	Ⓓ	Ⓔ
14	Ⓐ	Ⓑ	Ⓒ	Ⓓ	Ⓔ	69	Ⓐ	Ⓑ	Ⓒ	Ⓓ	Ⓔ	124	Ⓐ	Ⓑ	Ⓒ	Ⓓ	Ⓔ	179	Ⓐ	Ⓑ	Ⓒ	Ⓓ	Ⓔ
15	Ⓐ	Ⓑ	Ⓒ	Ⓓ	Ⓔ	70	Ⓐ	Ⓑ	Ⓒ	Ⓓ	Ⓔ	125	Ⓐ	Ⓑ	Ⓒ	Ⓓ	Ⓔ	180	Ⓐ	Ⓑ	Ⓒ	Ⓓ	Ⓔ
16	Ⓐ	Ⓑ	Ⓒ	Ⓓ	Ⓔ	71	Ⓐ	Ⓑ	Ⓒ	Ⓓ	Ⓔ	126	Ⓐ	Ⓑ	Ⓒ	Ⓓ	Ⓔ	181	Ⓐ	Ⓑ	Ⓒ	Ⓓ	Ⓔ
17	Ⓐ	Ⓑ	Ⓒ	Ⓓ	Ⓔ	72	Ⓐ	Ⓑ	Ⓒ	Ⓓ	Ⓔ	127	Ⓐ	Ⓑ	Ⓒ	Ⓓ	Ⓔ	182	Ⓐ	Ⓑ	Ⓒ	Ⓓ	Ⓔ
18	Ⓐ	Ⓑ	Ⓒ	Ⓓ	Ⓔ	73	Ⓐ	Ⓑ	Ⓒ	Ⓓ	Ⓔ	128	Ⓐ	Ⓑ	Ⓒ	Ⓓ	Ⓔ	183	Ⓐ	Ⓑ	Ⓒ	Ⓓ	Ⓔ
19	Ⓐ	Ⓑ	Ⓒ	Ⓓ	Ⓔ	74	Ⓐ	Ⓑ	Ⓒ	Ⓓ	Ⓔ	129	Ⓐ	Ⓑ	Ⓒ	Ⓓ	Ⓔ	184	Ⓐ	Ⓑ	Ⓒ	Ⓓ	Ⓔ
20	Ⓐ	Ⓑ	Ⓒ	Ⓓ	Ⓔ	75	Ⓐ	Ⓑ	Ⓒ	Ⓓ	Ⓔ	130	Ⓐ	Ⓑ	Ⓒ	Ⓓ	Ⓔ	185	Ⓐ	Ⓑ	Ⓒ	Ⓓ	Ⓔ
21	Ⓐ	Ⓑ	Ⓒ	Ⓓ	Ⓔ	76	Ⓐ	Ⓑ	Ⓒ	Ⓓ	Ⓔ	131	Ⓐ	Ⓑ	Ⓒ	Ⓓ	Ⓔ	186	Ⓐ	Ⓑ	Ⓒ	Ⓓ	Ⓔ
22	Ⓐ	Ⓑ	Ⓒ	Ⓓ	Ⓔ	77	Ⓐ	Ⓑ	Ⓒ	Ⓓ	Ⓔ	132	Ⓐ	Ⓑ	Ⓒ	Ⓓ	Ⓔ	187	Ⓐ	Ⓑ	Ⓒ	Ⓓ	Ⓔ
23	Ⓐ	Ⓑ	Ⓒ	Ⓓ	Ⓔ	78	Ⓐ	Ⓑ	Ⓒ	Ⓓ	Ⓔ	133	Ⓐ	Ⓑ	Ⓒ	Ⓓ	Ⓔ	188	Ⓐ	Ⓑ	Ⓒ	Ⓓ	Ⓔ
24	Ⓐ	Ⓑ	Ⓒ	Ⓓ	Ⓔ	79	Ⓐ	Ⓑ	Ⓒ	Ⓓ	Ⓔ	134	Ⓐ	Ⓑ	Ⓒ	Ⓓ	Ⓔ	189	Ⓐ	Ⓑ	Ⓒ	Ⓓ	Ⓔ
25	Ⓐ	Ⓑ	Ⓒ	Ⓓ	Ⓔ	80	Ⓐ	Ⓑ	Ⓒ	Ⓓ	Ⓔ	135	Ⓐ	Ⓑ	Ⓒ	Ⓓ	Ⓔ	190	Ⓐ	Ⓑ	Ⓒ	Ⓓ	Ⓔ
26	Ⓐ	Ⓑ	Ⓒ	Ⓓ	Ⓔ	81	Ⓐ	Ⓑ	Ⓒ	Ⓓ	Ⓔ	136	Ⓐ	Ⓑ	Ⓒ	Ⓓ	Ⓔ	191	Ⓐ	Ⓑ	Ⓒ	Ⓓ	Ⓔ
27	Ⓐ	Ⓑ	Ⓒ	Ⓓ	Ⓔ	82	Ⓐ	Ⓑ	Ⓒ	Ⓓ	Ⓔ	137	Ⓐ	Ⓑ	Ⓒ	Ⓓ	Ⓔ	192	Ⓐ	Ⓑ	Ⓒ	Ⓓ	Ⓔ
28	Ⓐ	Ⓑ	Ⓒ	Ⓓ	Ⓔ	83	Ⓐ	Ⓑ	Ⓒ	Ⓓ	Ⓔ	138	Ⓐ	Ⓑ	Ⓒ	Ⓓ	Ⓔ	193	Ⓐ	Ⓑ	Ⓒ	Ⓓ	Ⓔ
29	Ⓐ	Ⓑ	Ⓒ	Ⓓ	Ⓔ	84	Ⓐ	Ⓑ	Ⓒ	Ⓓ	Ⓔ	139	Ⓐ	Ⓑ	Ⓒ	Ⓓ	Ⓔ	194	Ⓐ	Ⓑ	Ⓒ	Ⓓ	Ⓔ
30	Ⓐ	Ⓑ	Ⓒ	Ⓓ	Ⓔ	85	Ⓐ	Ⓑ	Ⓒ	Ⓓ	Ⓔ	140	Ⓐ	Ⓑ	Ⓒ	Ⓓ	Ⓔ	195	Ⓐ	Ⓑ	Ⓒ	Ⓓ	Ⓔ
31	Ⓐ	Ⓑ	Ⓒ	Ⓓ	Ⓔ	86	Ⓐ	Ⓑ	Ⓒ	Ⓓ	Ⓔ	141	Ⓐ	Ⓑ	Ⓒ	Ⓓ	Ⓔ	196	Ⓐ	Ⓑ	Ⓒ	Ⓓ	Ⓔ
32	Ⓐ	Ⓑ	Ⓒ	Ⓓ	Ⓔ	87	Ⓐ	Ⓑ	Ⓒ	Ⓓ	Ⓔ	142	Ⓐ	Ⓑ	Ⓒ	Ⓓ	Ⓔ	197	Ⓐ	Ⓑ	Ⓒ	Ⓓ	Ⓔ
33	Ⓐ	Ⓑ	Ⓒ	Ⓓ	Ⓔ	88	Ⓐ	Ⓑ	Ⓒ	Ⓓ	Ⓔ	143	Ⓐ	Ⓑ	Ⓒ	Ⓓ	Ⓔ	198	Ⓐ	Ⓑ	Ⓒ	Ⓓ	Ⓔ
34	Ⓐ	Ⓑ	Ⓒ	Ⓓ	Ⓔ	89	Ⓐ	Ⓑ	Ⓒ	Ⓓ	Ⓔ	144	Ⓐ	Ⓑ	Ⓒ	Ⓓ	Ⓔ	199	Ⓐ	Ⓑ	Ⓒ	Ⓓ	Ⓔ
35	Ⓐ	Ⓑ	Ⓒ	Ⓓ	Ⓔ	90	Ⓐ	Ⓑ	Ⓒ	Ⓓ	Ⓔ	145	Ⓐ	Ⓑ	Ⓒ	Ⓓ	Ⓔ	200	Ⓐ	Ⓑ	Ⓒ	Ⓓ	Ⓔ
36	Ⓐ	Ⓑ	Ⓒ	Ⓓ	Ⓔ	91	Ⓐ	Ⓑ	Ⓒ	Ⓓ	Ⓔ	146	Ⓐ	Ⓑ	Ⓒ	Ⓓ	Ⓔ	201	Ⓐ	Ⓑ	Ⓒ	Ⓓ	Ⓔ
37	Ⓐ	Ⓑ	Ⓒ	Ⓓ	Ⓔ	92	Ⓐ	Ⓑ	Ⓒ	Ⓓ	Ⓔ	147	Ⓐ	Ⓑ	Ⓒ	Ⓓ	Ⓔ	202	Ⓐ	Ⓑ	Ⓒ	Ⓓ	Ⓔ
38	Ⓐ	Ⓑ	Ⓒ	Ⓓ	Ⓔ	93	Ⓐ	Ⓑ	Ⓒ	Ⓓ	Ⓔ	148	Ⓐ	Ⓑ	Ⓒ	Ⓓ	Ⓔ	203	Ⓐ	Ⓑ	Ⓒ	Ⓓ	Ⓔ
39	Ⓐ	Ⓑ	Ⓒ	Ⓓ	Ⓔ	94	Ⓐ	Ⓑ	Ⓒ	Ⓓ	Ⓔ	149	Ⓐ	Ⓑ	Ⓒ	Ⓓ	Ⓔ	204	Ⓐ	Ⓑ	Ⓒ	Ⓓ	Ⓔ
40	Ⓐ	Ⓑ	Ⓒ	Ⓓ	Ⓔ	95	Ⓐ	Ⓑ	Ⓒ	Ⓓ	Ⓔ	150	Ⓐ	Ⓑ	Ⓒ	Ⓓ	Ⓔ	205	Ⓐ	Ⓑ	Ⓒ	Ⓓ	Ⓔ
41	Ⓐ	Ⓑ	Ⓒ	Ⓓ	Ⓔ	96	Ⓐ	Ⓑ	Ⓒ	Ⓓ	Ⓔ	151	Ⓐ	Ⓑ	Ⓒ	Ⓓ	Ⓔ	206	Ⓐ	Ⓑ	Ⓒ	Ⓓ	Ⓔ
42	Ⓐ	Ⓑ	Ⓒ	Ⓓ	Ⓔ	97	Ⓐ	Ⓑ	Ⓒ	Ⓓ	Ⓔ	152	Ⓐ	Ⓑ	Ⓒ	Ⓓ	Ⓔ	207	Ⓐ	Ⓑ	Ⓒ	Ⓓ	Ⓔ
43	Ⓐ	Ⓑ	Ⓒ	Ⓓ	Ⓔ	98	Ⓐ	Ⓑ	Ⓒ	Ⓓ	Ⓔ	153	Ⓐ	Ⓑ	Ⓒ	Ⓓ	Ⓔ	208	Ⓐ	Ⓑ	Ⓒ	Ⓓ	Ⓔ
44	Ⓐ	Ⓑ	Ⓒ	Ⓓ	Ⓔ	99	Ⓐ	Ⓑ	Ⓒ	Ⓓ	Ⓔ	154	Ⓐ	Ⓑ	Ⓒ	Ⓓ	Ⓔ	209	Ⓐ	Ⓑ	Ⓒ	Ⓓ	Ⓔ
45	Ⓐ	Ⓑ	Ⓒ	Ⓓ	Ⓔ	100	Ⓐ	Ⓑ	Ⓒ	Ⓓ	Ⓔ	155	Ⓐ	Ⓑ	Ⓒ	Ⓓ	Ⓔ	210	Ⓐ	Ⓑ	Ⓒ	Ⓓ	Ⓔ
46	Ⓐ	Ⓑ	Ⓒ	Ⓓ	Ⓔ	101	Ⓐ	Ⓑ	Ⓒ	Ⓓ	Ⓔ	156	Ⓐ	Ⓑ	Ⓒ	Ⓓ	Ⓔ	211	Ⓐ	Ⓑ	Ⓒ	Ⓓ	Ⓔ
47	Ⓐ	Ⓑ	Ⓒ	Ⓓ	Ⓔ	102	Ⓐ	Ⓑ	Ⓒ	Ⓓ	Ⓔ	157	Ⓐ	Ⓑ	Ⓒ	Ⓓ	Ⓔ	212	Ⓐ	Ⓑ	Ⓒ	Ⓓ	Ⓔ
48	Ⓐ	Ⓑ	Ⓒ	Ⓓ	Ⓔ	103	Ⓐ	Ⓑ	Ⓒ	Ⓓ	Ⓔ	158	Ⓐ	Ⓑ	Ⓒ	Ⓓ	Ⓔ	213	Ⓐ	Ⓑ	Ⓒ	Ⓓ	Ⓔ
49	Ⓐ	Ⓑ	Ⓒ	Ⓓ	Ⓔ	104	Ⓐ	Ⓑ	Ⓒ	Ⓓ	Ⓔ	159	Ⓐ	Ⓑ	Ⓒ	Ⓓ	Ⓔ	214	Ⓐ	Ⓑ	Ⓒ	Ⓓ	Ⓔ
50	Ⓐ	Ⓑ	Ⓒ	Ⓓ	Ⓔ	105	Ⓐ	Ⓑ	Ⓒ	Ⓓ	Ⓔ	160	Ⓐ	Ⓑ	Ⓒ	Ⓓ	Ⓔ	215	Ⓐ	Ⓑ	Ⓒ	Ⓓ	Ⓔ
51	Ⓐ	Ⓑ	Ⓒ	Ⓓ	Ⓔ	106	Ⓐ	Ⓑ	Ⓒ	Ⓓ	Ⓔ	161	Ⓐ	Ⓑ	Ⓒ	Ⓓ	Ⓔ						
52	Ⓐ	Ⓑ	Ⓒ	Ⓓ	Ⓔ	107	Ⓐ	Ⓑ	Ⓒ	Ⓓ	Ⓔ	162	Ⓐ	Ⓑ	Ⓒ	Ⓓ	Ⓔ						
53	Ⓐ	Ⓑ	Ⓒ	Ⓓ	Ⓔ	108	Ⓐ	Ⓑ	Ⓒ	Ⓓ	Ⓔ	163	Ⓐ	Ⓑ	Ⓒ	Ⓓ	Ⓔ						
54	Ⓐ	Ⓑ	Ⓒ	Ⓓ	Ⓔ	109	Ⓐ	Ⓑ	Ⓒ	Ⓓ	Ⓔ	164	Ⓐ	Ⓑ	Ⓒ	Ⓓ	Ⓔ						
55	Ⓐ	Ⓑ	Ⓒ	Ⓓ	Ⓔ	110	Ⓐ	Ⓑ	Ⓒ	Ⓓ	Ⓔ	165	Ⓐ	Ⓑ	Ⓒ	Ⓓ	Ⓔ						

NOTES

NOTES

NOTES

NOTES

NOTES

NOTES

NOTES